THE MUSIC GODS ARE REAL VOLUME 1

The MUSIC GODS *are* REAL

Vol. 1: THE ROAD *to* THE SHOW

JONATHAN A. FINK

The Music Gods are Real: Volume 1 - The Road to the Show

Written by Jonathan A. Fink
Copyright 2020

Polo Grounds Publishing LLC

No part of this publication may be reproduced, stored in a retrieval system or transmitted in any form by any means, electronic, mechanical, photocopying or otherwise, without the prior written permission of Jonathan A. Fink.

Credit and thank you to Meg Reid for Book Cover Design and Book Layout

Credit and thank you to Meg Schader for Editing

Credit and thank you to Kim Watson for my Biography Picture

Credit and thank you to Abi Laksono for Polo Grounds Publishing Logo

Thank you to my Mom and Dad, Beth and Jeffrey Fink, for their help, guidance, support and unconditional love.

And thank you to my wife, Reggie, and my kids, Kayla and Nate, for their love, patience, understanding and support.

This book is dedicated to Matthew Laconti, Hattibagen McRat

TABLE OF CONTENTS

The Introduction	1
Chapter 1: The Jamflowman	5
Chapter 2: The Glory Days	9
Chapter 3: The Born in the USA Tour	12
Chapter 4: The Tulane Years	21
Chapter 5: The Grateful Dead	31
Chapter 6: The Patti Rothberg Experience	35
Chapter 7: The Primitive Radio Gods	41
Chapter 8: The Scarecrow Collection	44
Chapter 9: The Black Crowes	51
Chapter 10: The Year Phish Became Phish	57
Chapter 11: The Clifford Ball	63
Chapter 12: The Year Phish Broke Up	65
Chapter 13: The Great Gatsby	67
Chapter 14: The Promised Land	71
Chapter 15: The Torch	78
Chapter 16: The Dolores Cannon Method	90
Chapter 17: The Road to Montana	94
Chapter 18: The Winter Tour	100
Chapter 19: The recordBar Prophecy	106
Chapter 20: The Vision Quest	113
Chapter 21: The Road to Red Rocks	126
The Conclusion	151

THE INTRODUCTION

MY FIRST BOOK, *THE BASEBALL GODS ARE REAL: A TRUE Story About Baseball and Spirituality*, was published in 2018. It chronicled the first part of my life, from elementary school through college, and described some of my earliest professional career experiences. It also recounted my midlife crisis at age 38, which inspired me to explore a spiritual path and described how I transformed myself through a practice of yoga and meditation. It also awakened in me the desire to share my thoughts, beliefs and experiences with others. That's when I started a second career as an author, my first being a financial and investment advisor as President of Satya Investment Management, the asset management company I founded in 2016.

During this transformative process, I was introduced to the Baseball Gods, a term used to explain the mysterious and coincidental events that so often occur in the world of baseball. My recently published second book, *The Baseball Gods are Real - Volume 2: The Road to the Show*, expanded on the Baseball Gods theme as I travelled to ballparks all across America telling stories about some famous and not so famous ballplayers, ballparks and historic baseball events.

Interwoven throughout my first Baseball Gods book, I often referenced music. The book even featured a chapter entitled "The Music Industry Years" in which I describe my life-long passion for music. For me, this began at an early age. When I was just a toddler, I would listen to the music my parents loved and blasted through the speakers in the living room of my childhood home in Merrick, Long Island in New York. As a kid, I grew up listening to Bruce Springsteen & the E Street Band, the Oak Ridge Boys, John Denver and the Eagles. As a teenager I progressed to rap, hair bands and hard rock. In college I advanced to jambands like Phish, Widespread Panic and the Grateful Dead.

My first gig in the music business was at a Record World store on Merrick Road in Bellmore. I worked there part-time during my senior year at John F. Kennedy High School, in between my schoolwork and student government activities as senior class president. Then in college at Tulane University in New Orleans, my passion for music grew exponentially. I became a disc jockey at the college radio station. I joined the staff of *The Hullabaloo*, the campus newspaper, and reviewed new music albums. I frequented popular music venues and saw countless live performances by local and well-known touring bands. I reviewed these shows for *The Hullabaloo* as well. During the summer after my sophomore year, I worked as an intern in the marketing department of EMI Records in New

THE MUSIC GODS ARE REAL VOL. 1

York City. For the next two years, I was employed on a part-time basis for EMI Records as a regional sales representative in New Orleans. And after graduating from Tulane, my first post-college employment was in the music industry. I worked as an assistant to Alicia Gelernt, who at the time managed the career of up-and-coming EMI Records recording artist Patti Rothberg. I loved every minute of it.

I plan to continue to manage and expand Satya Investment Management. I also plan to pen additional books in my series related to baseball and spirituality. However, I felt it was time to add a new book series to my Polo Grounds Publishing company's catalogue. The first book in this series, *The Music Gods are Real: Volume 1. - The Road to the Show*, accomplishes this objective. In this book, I share stories and events related to my first true love — music.

I take my readers along for the ride on the road to the show using music, rather than baseball, as the vehicle. The road is the metaphor for the path of life. The show is a metaphor for the life goals people strive to reach, such as a student earning his or her college degree, a minor league baseball player making it to the major leagues, or a rock and roll band playing at the music venue of their dreams, like the Red Rocks Amphitheatre in Morrison, Colorado, or Madison Square Garden in New York City. The road to the show stories in this book feature several bands and recording artists including Bruce Springsteen & the E Street Band, the Grateful Dead, Phish, Widespread Panic, Mumford & Sons, the Black Crowes, the Counting Crowes, Scarecrow Collection, Primitive Radio Gods, Patti Rothberg, Russ, the Wiggles, Pigeons Playing Ping Pong, the Kitchen Dwellers, Iya Terra and Twiddle.

JONATHAN FINK

Music has that special something. It has the ability to stimulate your mind, open your heart, lift your spirits, produce tears and laughter and feed your soul. Music can make you feel alive. Music can make you feel born again. I hope you love reading this book and conclude, like I did, that the Music Gods are real!

CHAPTER ONE

The Jamflowman

"No place to go but everywhere"
— Dispatch

MOST PEOPLE REMEMBER THE TIME WHEN THEY WERE introduced to music and the love affair began. For some the path was straight, as it was for Mihali Savoulidis, the lead singer and guitarist for the Vermont-based jamband Twiddle. Mihali was raised in a small town in New Jersey. He loved skateboarding and soccer. His liberal, open-minded parents encouraged their son to listen to all kinds of music including blues, jazz, reggae and rock and roll. By the age of ten, Mihali was learning to play the guitar. At fourteen, he wrote his first song entitled "Invisible Ink."

Although just a teenager, "Invisible Ink" reveals Mihali's brilliant musical mind with his catchy melodies and insightful lyrics. The song has a fun, upbeat reggae rhythm that just makes the listener feel joyful and happy. Yet, the lyrics showcase the wisdom of an old soul, expressing regret, personal

JONATHAN FINK

transformation and perseverance. The chorus is particularly instructive and gives listeners a lot to think about:

> Don't you wish you were a pencil so you could erase
> the shit you've done.
> Go back and make the changes and control
> how your life's run.
> Cause people make mistakes and people do things
> that they shouldn't have done.
> Go back and make the changes and replace them
> with some fun.

In his freshman year of high school, Mihali was already carefully planning his road to the show by applying to colleges in Vermont and starting his own band. He accepted the first college offer he received, from Castleton University in beautiful Castleton, VT. Mihali's master plan was coming together.

For others the path was not so straight. Ryan Dempsey, Twiddle's keyboard player, grew up in a small town in Vermont. He was homeschooled. His religious parents encouraged music, but certain music deemed a bad influence was forbidden. Ryan's childhood was sheltered from bands like the Rolling Stones, Led Zeppelin, AC/DC, Guns N' Roses, Pink Floyd and the Grateful Dead. The only mainstream music played in the Dempsey household was the Beatles. When Ryan discovered his passion for the piano, he did not start by learning sheet music for songs like "Sympathy for the Devil" by the Rolling Stones. Instead, he grew up on classical music and Ryan's road to the show began by practicing Beethoven. At some point, Ryan found his way from Beethoven to Phish.

THE MUSIC GODS ARE REAL VOL. 1

Savoulidis and Dempsey clearly had different paths on their road to the show. However, their love of music brought them together and led them to the same place at the same time to form their band — Twiddle.

I had a different path. I grew up in the small town of Merrick on Long Island in New York. As a kid, I loved baseball, karate and music. My mom, Beth Fink, was an elementary school teacher and I remember listening to music with her all the time. Our favorite album was *Mommy Gimme a Drinka Water* by Danny Kaye. My dad, Jeffrey Fink, was an attorney and a CPA who loved sports, investing and music. As a kid, I recall him coming home late from a long day of work. After dinner sometimes, he would lie down on the floor next to the large speakers in our living room and listen to his favorite music. Many times, I would crawl up on his back and listen with him. Looking back now, as a spiritual person who practices yoga and meditation on a daily basis, I realize that listening to music while lying on the living room floor in the dark was my dad's form of meditation and relaxation.

Music was playing all the time in my childhood home and the radio was always blasting during family car trips and vacations. Many times, my dad would sing along with the lyrics to his favorite songs while driving. He introduced me to great recording artists such as Abba, Fleetwood Mac, Bob Seger and his Silver Bullet Band, Creedence Clearwater Revival, folk singers Cat Stevens and Peter, Paul & Mary and country icons Alabama and Garth Brooks. But no artist blasted through our living room speakers more often or louder than Bruce Springsteen & the E Street Band, my dad's favorite band. When my father passed down his love for music to me, I began

7

my own music road to the show. I would soon become — The Jamflowman.

CHAPTER TWO

The Glory Days

"I saw rock and roll future, and its name is Bruce Springsteen."
—Jon Landau

THE SEEDS OF MY APPRECIATION FOR LIVE MUSIC WERE
planted long before I fell in love with jambands like Phish and
Widespread Panic. Of all the recording artists and bands that
my dad introduced me to during my childhood, one stood out
from all the rest — Bruce Springsteen & the E Street Band. To
this day, after attending hundreds of truly great live performances by dozens of fabulously talented bands, few have
matched the energy and electricity of a Bruce Springsteen
concert.

Like Mihali Savoulidis from Twiddle, Bruce Springsteen
was born in a small New Jersey town. His mother had a full-
time job as a legal secretary and his father worked various
jobs between periods of unemployment. Springsteen attended
Catholic school where he frequently rebelled against the
powers that be. Interestingly, before the age of 15, Springsteen's
passion was not music. It was actually baseball.

9

During many of his over three-hour-long concerts, Springsteen describes his childhood baseball experiences. This typically leads into one of his most popular songs, the anthem "Glory Days." I love this song because of its baseball theme and the nostalgic, somewhat painful story it tells about recapturing the past. In the song, two old friends run into each other at a roadside bar and talk about their glory days playing high school baseball together.

Like John Fogerty's song "Centerfield," Springsteen's "Glory Days" has become iconic and synonymous with the game of baseball. Both songs are played all the time at baseball stadiums across the country. During his live shows, Springsteen narrates his childhood baseball story with a quintessential humble and self-deprecating sense of humor. He discusses climbing the baseball ranks from Little League to the Babe Ruth League and then to high school baseball. However, in high school Bruce discovered the guitar and his love of music and storytelling. Music would slowly and then abruptly replace his love of baseball.

It was at that time that Springsteen's mom agreed to rent a guitar for her son. She rented rather than purchased because doing so was less expensive and she wasn't sure whether Bruce would truly focus and stick with this new hobby. It didn't take long for Bruce to realize how difficult it was to learn to play and he wanted to quit just as his mom feared might happen.

Despite this setback Bruce was not deterred. He tried even harder to learn to play the guitar and his passion for music continued to grow. After some time and many hours of practice, he learned to play well enough and started writing songs. A few years later, and considerably more confident in

THE MUSIC GODS ARE REAL VOL. 1

his musical ability, Bruce was on stage showcasing his songs in small, local venues. Playing baseball during the day and performing on stage at night was working out well for Bruce, so he did this for a while.

One day a game that Bruce's baseball team was scheduled to play got rained out. Unfortunately, the makeup game was rescheduled for early Saturday morning. That created a problem for Bruce. He had played a show the night before, had made it home and into bed just before sunrise and the next thing he knew his teammates were knocking on his front door to wake him up for the game. As the story goes, Bruce told his mom to tell his teammates that he was sick and could not play. The truth was that Bruce was seriously hungover from a night of rocking and rolling and drinking. After departing Springsteen's house, the team realized they had only eight players and needed Bruce to play or they would forfeit the game. The team marched right back to the Springsteen house and begged Bruce to get out of bed to play in the game.

Springsteen played right field that day and probably prayed that no balls would be hit his way. The Baseball Gods were kind to Bruce and for eight innings there was no action in right field. However, the Music Gods had a different plan for him. They wanted to help Bruce on his music road to the show, so they intervened. In the ninth inning, a deep, towering fly ball was hit to right field. Bruce, tired, hungover and half asleep from a night of performing and drinking, botched the play and the other team scored the winning run. Perhaps it was destiny or the Music Gods pulling the strings, but at that very moment, Bruce's baseball career ended and his music road to the show began.

CHAPTER THREE

The Born in the USA Tour

"This was different, shifted the lay of the land. Four guys, playing and singing, writing their own material... Rock 'n' roll came to my house where there seemed to be no way out...and opened up a whole world of possibilities."

— Bruce Springsteen

LEGEND HAS IT THAT THE ROAD TO THE SHOW FOR Bruce Springsteen actually began when he was seven years old, not as a teenager when he got his first guitar. That's when he saw Elvis Presley on television on the *Ed Sullivan Show*. Years later in February of 1964, Springsteen, like millions of other Americans, including thousands of screaming teenage girls, got to see the Beatles perform, also on the *Ed Sullivan Show*. The Music Gods had finally gotten to Bruce Springsteen. Shortly after the Beatles sang "I Want to Hold Your Hand" before the then largest TV audience ever in the US, Springsteen bought his first guitar at the Western Auto Appliance store near his home in Freehold, New Jersey. This was a much better and more expensive guitar than the one his mom had rented for him years before.

THE MUSIC GODS ARE REAL VOL. 1

Like almost all performers and bands in the music business, Springsteen struggled in his early years to make a name for himself. During this difficult and disappointing period, he played guitar and sang vocals in several unsuccessful bands. He was searching for the right fit and hadn't found it yet. Then, in 1971, Springsteen joined forces with some local musicians from the Asbury Park, New Jersey, music scene to form what would eventual become the E Street Band. He knew right away, this was it.

Bruce played guitar and added the harmonica to his E Street Band repertoire. The band developed a unique sound that blended blues, R&B, jazz, soul and early rock and roll. Springsteen acquired the nickname "The Boss" because he was in charge of collecting the band's nightly pay for each gig and distributing the cash to each of the band members. And it was clear to all that on stage, he was the one in control. It was also clear that the band was getting better and better with each performance.

It was a proud day for Bruce Springsteen & the E Street Band when they signed a deal with Columbia Records after being discovered by Clive Davis, its legendary artist & repertoire division executive. After playing trailer parks, bowling alleys and other small local venues for years, Springsteen thought this record deal would accelerate his road to the show. However, that proved not to be the case. The band's debut album, *Greetings from Asbury Park, N.J.*, was released in January 1973 and while it received some critical acclaim, sales were sluggish and unimpressive. Their second album, *The Wild, The Innocent & the E Street Shuffle*, released later that year in September, was a commercial failure. Springsteen's

JONATHAN FINK

career and road to the show got off to a slow and rocky start, like a car with a bad engine and four bald tires, and he faced an uncertain future in the music business.

However, Springsteen refused to give up on his dream. He took a realistic look at his strengths and shortcomings and decided to make changes to improve his situation. First, the band decided to switch managers. After a long legal dispute with their record label, the band parted ways with their manager. Then, in May of 1974, they hired Jon Landau, a loyal fan, to handle the band's affairs going forward. This relationship still exists to this day. In addition, Bruce realized that in order to get to the next level, he needed a better band. While he was a great performer, songwriter and band leader, Bruce knew he was not the greatest guitar soloist. So, putting ego aside, he recruited a guitar playing virtuoso, Steven Van Zandt, to join the band. Then he recruited a saxophone playing virtuoso, Clarence "The Big Man" Clemons, who also agreed to join the band. Now, with these two truly talented new musicians on board, Springsteen was ready to get the E Street Band out of neutral and put the pedal to the metal. The engine was all tuned up and the car was fully equipped with a new set of all-season radial tires.

During the months that the E. Street Band was in a legal dispute with their former manager and record label, they were not permitted to record in the studio. Instead, they toured relentlessly. Springsteen and his bandmates were quietly becoming the greatest band you've never heard of. While the E Street Band was not achieving commercial success or getting any radio play during this period of time, they developed a loyal following on the road playing enthusiastic, hand

14

THE MUSIC GODS ARE REAL VOL. 1

clapping, foot stomping, extremely entertaining, four-hour shows. The buzz surrounding the band continued to grow as they toured the country. And when they returned home in the summer of 1975, they did something that increased their visibility tremendously and changed the live performance music scene forever.

Springsteen & the E Street Band played a five-night, ten-show run at the Bottom Line in New York City. This week-long run attracted significant media attention and was broadcast live on the radio. Years later, *Rolling Stone* magazine included this historic musical event as one of "The 50 Moments That Changed Rock and Roll." Phish, the great jamband who recently played seventeen straight sold out shows at Madison Square Garden, has Bruce Springsteen & the E Street Band to thank for breaking new ground and setting the stage, so to speak, for them and many others. Now, two-, three-, and four-night stands are common for touring bands when they play big cities.

Commercial success finally found Springsteen & the E Street Band with their next album, *Born to Run*, which reached #3 on the *Billboard* 200 charts. The lead song of the same title, "*Born to Run*," along with "Thunder Road" and "Jungleland" became legendary rock anthems for the band's live shows. *Born to Run* sold more than 6 million copies in the U.S. and millions more worldwide. Three years later in 1978, after extensive touring and resolved contractual obligations, Springsteen released the album *Darkness on the Edge of Town*.

Bruce Springsteen's much awaited fourth album received extremely positive reviews and high praise from fans. In

JONATHAN FINK

2003, *Rolling Stone* magazine ranked it at #151 on its greatest albums of all-time list. Then in 1980, Springsteen released his 20-song, double album entitled *The River*. This album included the song "Hungry Heart," Springsteen's first top ten single. The album made it to #1 on the U.S. pop chart, also a first for Springsteen. Years later as a teenager, I listened to these albums in my room over and over and over again. Just like my parents, I was hooked on — The Boss.

Springsteen followed up his consecutive run of rock and roll based albums in 1982 with *Nebraska*, an acoustic album he recorded on a simple, low-tech four-track tape on his front porch. *Nebraska* includes one of my all-time favorite songs, "Atlantic City." The lyrics include the line "Everything dies baby, that's a fact, but maybe everything that dies someday comes back." Bruce was probably referring to the city. Perhaps he was also referring to reincarnation. Only Bruce and the Music Gods know for sure.

By 1984, Bruce Springsteen & the E Street Band were no longer "the greatest band you've never heard of." Now it was the greatest band everyone had heard of. Springsteen had become a music icon and a household name. He had made it to the show, both on stage with concert sales and in the studio with record sales. And on top of all this, the best was yet to come. His next album, *Born in the U.S.A.*, became one of the best-selling albums of all time, with seven singles hitting the Top 10 on the *Billboard* charts and more than 30 million albums sold worldwide. The record received an Album of the Year nomination at the 1985 Grammy Awards and Bruce won his first Grammy for Record of the Year (single) for his song "Dancing in the Dark."

THE MUSIC GODS ARE REAL VOL. 1

Bruce Springsteen recorded many great albums over the years, but, in my opinion, the E Street Band was at its very best performing live on stage. So, with the biggest album in the world, it was only natural for the band to follow it up with the biggest tour in the world. Long gone were the trailer parks, bowling alleys and small, 400-person capacity clubs. The E Street Band began the *Born in the U.S.A.* Tour in the United States playing large venues and arenas. And when they returned home a year later, they were playing to sold out crowds at football stadiums!

The *Born in the U.S.A.* Tour began on June 29, 1984 and ended more than a year later in October of 1985. It had four legs and spanned four continents. The band played an incredible total of 155 shows, 121 in North America, 8 in Australia, 8 in Asia and 18 Europe. The tour grossed more than $80 million and almost four million people saw the band perform in person.

The tour was both exhilarating and exhausting. Unlike most touring bands, Bruce Springsteen & the E Street Band played a different setlist every night. When they performed at Giants Stadium at the Meadowlands in their home state of New Jersey for the first time ever, they played multiple nights in a row. Springsteen created a different setlist for each performance, adding new songs and eliminating others. As a result, many die-hard Bruce fans attended each and every show of the run because they knew every performance would be different each night.

I have some wonderful personal memories of Bruce Springsteen & the E Street Band. When the band returned to New Jersey for their run of multiple shows at Giants Stadium

JONATHAN FINK

after touring the world, I was there for one of them. My parents were anxious to see Springsteen in person and they took my sister Jamie and I along for the ride. Even though I was only ten years old at the time, I can still vividly recall so many details about that performance. I remember where our seats were located. I remember the noise level in the stadium. I remember waiting with great anticipation to see which song the band would open with and which song they would play next throughout the concert. By the way, they opened the show with "Born in the U.S.A," as many screaming fans in the stands were hoping.

While Springsteen & the E Street Band were off stage taking a short break between encores, fans in the upper deck of the stadium cheered as loud as they could in unison for the band to play "Jungleland." I remember screaming as loud as I could right along with the crowd. However, when Springsteen and the band came out for their last of several encores, they played "Rosalita," another Bruce classic. Some fans were disappointed while others were elated. At that moment, even at such a young age, I was impressed with the genius of a band that could play a different setlist every night and keep their fans on the edge of their seats waiting with anticipation for the next song they would perform.

Shortly after that concert, I had a check-up appointment to see my pediatrician, Dr. Daniel Minor. That was when I learned that Dr. Minor loved Bruce Springsteen even more than my folks. I will never forget the time he told my dad in front of me that he had just seen Bruce play six shows in a row, and that this wasn't the first time he had done that. Dr. Minor's love for music made a big impression on me. It

18

showed me that a person could have an important job, like a physician, yet love music so much that, even as an adult, it was ok to see the same band play multiple nights in a row. Like Dr. Minor, I am still as passionate today about music as I was as a teenager even though I am a financial advisor running my own investment company and an author as well. Dr. Minor, thank you and may the Music Gods always be with you.

That wasn't the only time I had the pleasure to see Bruce Springsteen & the E Street Band perform live and dance through a fabulous four-hour concert. Many years later, my wife and I, along with my sister Jamie and brother-in-law Brian, took our mom and dad to see the band at Giants Stadium to celebrate their fortieth wedding anniversary. That evening my folks were truly kids again, singing along with Bruce and the crowd, stomping their feet to the beat of music. What a special night that was for all of us. More recently in 2018, I took my son, Nate, to see Bruce Springsteen and the E Street Band at the Sprint Center in Kansas City. That was another special evening for me. Nate seemed to enjoy this live performance as much as I did. In addition, the experience added another memorable event to our growing catalogue of father-son adventures.

Without a doubt, Bruce Springsteen had made it on his road to the show. For Springsteen and his bandmates, the *Born in the U.S.A.* Tour became a temporal marker in their rise to superstardom. Many more successful albums and tours would follow. The *Born in the U.S.A.* Tour was an important stepping stone to a long, hugely successful music career. To date, Springsteen has sold more than 135 million albums worldwide. He has won many awards for his music, including twenty Grammys, two Golden Globes, an Academy Award and, recently, a Tony Award for his *Springsteen on Broadway* performance. He was inducted into the Songwriters Hall of Fame and the Rock and Roll Hall of Fame and received a Kennedy Center Honor in 2009. Quite a record of outstanding musical achievement.

I need to send out a very special thank you to Bruce Springsteen & the E Street Band. I can't begin to count the many hours of pleasure I have enjoyed listening to your music. Also, by attending my first Springsteen concert at Giants Stadium many, many years ago as a ten-year old kid, you planted the seed for my deep appreciation of live performance music. Bruce Springsteen and the E Street Band, may the Music Gods always be with you!

CHAPTER FOUR

The Tulane Years

"A tree of knowledge in your soul will grow."
—Phish

I CAME INTO THE WORLD LISTENING TO THE MUSIC MY parents loved — Springsteen, Abba, the Eagles and a lot of country music. As a teenager in junior high and high school, making my own decisions, I explored several different genres of music. During my rap and hip-hop phase, I listened to Run-DMC and the Beastie Boys. When I went through my hair band stage, I listened to rock bands like Van Halen, Guns n' Roses and Poison. I would go to see their concerts at the Nassau Coliseum in Hempstead, Long Island with my friends, with mom or dad as a chaperon, mostly with my mom. During my senior year of high school, when I had my part-time job at Record World, I went through a grunge rock phase. I listened mostly to Pearl Jam, with some Nirvana and Soundgarden thrown into the mix. Then, my friend Mark Weinberg, who also worked at Record World, invited me to join him and his buddy Matthew Sector to see a band called the Spin Doctors.

JONATHAN FINK

The Spin Doctors were one of the first jambands that emerged out of the shadows of the Grateful Dead era. My first Spin Doctors show was awesome. The band was not well known yet, but you could tell from the energy of the crowd and the vibe at the venue that this band was on its road to the show. They sang funky songs like "Yo Mama's A Pajama." The band eventually signed with Epic Records in 1991. Best known for their early 1990's hit songs "Two Princes" and "Little Miss Can't Be Wrong," the group is still together and continues to tour.

Then I discovered the amazing harmonica player and singer John Popper when I saw his band Blues Traveler play a show at The Wetlands in downtown NYC. That night Blues Traveler shared the stage with the Spin Doctors. The group founded the H.O.R.D.E. festival and earned a Grammy for its upbeat pop single "Run-Around." The band still performs and John Popper remains one of the most recognizable personalities in the music industry today. By the end of my senior year of high school, I was hooked on jambands. My friends and I would spend many Friday nights driving from Merrick to Freeport to see the Grateful Dead cover band called the Zen Tricksters.

During my junior year in high school, I started visiting college campuses with my parents to find a university that would be a good fit for me after graduation. At the top of my list was Tulane University, a relatively small, private school in New Orleans with an excellent reputation and a NCAA Division I sports programs. We found time between campus tours to visit the famous French Quarter and after my first glimpse of the New Orleans music scene, I knew that Tulane was the place for me.

22

My love of music and jambands came with me to New Orleans during my four years in college. The city's local music scene was filled with live improvisational jazz, funk and blues bands. Downtown on or near Bourbon Street or uptown near Tulane's campus, a great band was playing great music somewhere every night of the week. For example, the famous Maple Leaf Bar on Oak Street in uptown New Orleans might have a local upstart brass funk quartet on stage, while downtown in the French Quarter you could find seasoned acts like the Preservation Hall Jazz Band doing their thing. My favorite bands while at Tulane were the Meters, Galactic, the Neville Brothers, the Radiators and George Porter Jr.'s sideband called the Runnin' Pardners. While all these bands had slightly different styles, what they had in common was a foundation in improvisational music, also known as "jamming."

My affection for the jamband music scene was codified the first semester of my freshman year at Tulane in 1992. The club was Tipitina's. The band was — Widespread Panic. Initially formed in 1986 by singer John Bell and his friend Michael Houser in their dorm room at the University of Georgia, the band had recently signed with Capricorn Records. Shortly thereafter they released their debut album entitled *Widespread Panic*. During this show the band showcased a few songs from this new album along with some fan favorites. Here is the setlist from what was for me a truly outstanding, eye-opening, live performance, which made me a life-long Widespread Panic fan.

Widespread Panic: 10/26/92 - Tipitina's, New Orleans, LA

I: Driving Song>Hatfield>Driving Song>Love Tractor,

JONATHAN FINK

Worry, I'm Not Alone, It Ain't No Use>Dream
Song>Weight of the World, Send Your Mind>Walkin' (For
Your Love), Diner, Space Wrangler, Chilly Water

E: The Take Out>Porch Song

A setlist is the list, in order, of the songs to be performed
during each set of a concert. "I" references set one, "II" references set two, and so on. "E" references the encore. A comma
indicates a song is completed. However, if a band "jams"
from one song to another without stopping, or "segues" or
"jams their way" into another song, a "greater than" symbol
(>) references the transition. Sometimes a setlist shows a "full
arrow" (->) which represents that a jam at the end of the previous song seamlessly segued into the next song.

Widespread Panic opened the show with "Driving Song."
It's a slow building song that lasted almost ten minutes and
took full advantage of the band's six pieces, especially the
chimes played by their great percussionist Domingo "Sunny"
Ortiz. John Bell sang the lyrics and the first verse in particular
stayed with me:

The leaves seen through my window pane,
remind me that it's time to move my life again.
November sun is felt by none,
a chilly breeze has blown my thoughts to what's to come.

These thoughtful words and the unique sound of the band
had me mesmerized. Like a subtle, chilly breeze on a sunny

THE MUSIC GODS ARE REAL VOL. 1

November day, the band segued into "Hatfield," a song about the rain-making skills of Mr. Charles Hatfield.

For background, Charles Hatfield was born in Kansas before moving to Southern California where he was employed as a sewing machine salesman. His hobby was chemistry and in his spare time, he loved to experiment. In the early 1900s, Hatfield mixed some chemicals together to see if it was possible to make rain. Hatfield's invention, which he called "a moisture accelerator," actually succeeded. While he was accused of pseudoscience at that time, his discovery was the early predecessor to "cloud seeding," which gave birth to today's weather modification or "geoengineering industry."

Hatfield travelled the country selling his rain-making services. As a marketing strategy, he told customers that he would not collect a cent for his efforts unless he produced results. He did, and as he had more and more success making rain with his invention, he started raising his fee. His reputation grew to such an extent that the city of San Diego, California, hired him to fill up a large reservoir to offset the adverse effects of the severe drought the community was experiencing. At first, the citizens of San Diego were overjoyed and grateful for the rain. They believed that their prayers had been answered. However, the rain kept coming down in buckets, so much so that the reservoir overflowed, the dams broke and the city flooded. The resulting damage was extensive with flooding so severe that 20 people lost their lives. Hatfield didn't stay in San Diego to collect his fee. He left town in fear for his life and took his moisture accelerator with him.

Back to the Widespread Panic show where I remained immersed in the song, I again heard Sunny and his chimes.

JONATHAN FINK

The band began to slow down and soften the music, almost to a gentle whisper, and they segued back into "Driving Song." I had never seen or heard a band mesh two songs together like that, playing one song, then a different song, then returning to the first song to finish the un-played verses. Having been to hundreds of concerts since my college days at Tulane, I can report that many jambands now do this regularly during their live performances.

Later in the show, I sensed the crowd falling into a dreamlike state when Widespread Panic performed "Dream Song," a beautiful lullaby the band rarely performs. The band ended the show with two of their most beloved songs, "Space Wrangler" and "Chilly Water." These songs seemed to bring the audience to a state of euphoria. After several minutes of applause and cheering, the band returned to the stage for their encore and peaked once again while performing "The Take Out" and "Porch Song." My friends and I stumbled out of Tipitina's that night feeling like we all just had a religious experience.

I was truly impressed with the raw talent of Widespread Panic, their musicianship, their setlist creativity, and the way they captured the crowd. I guess that's why the group has remained one of my favorite bands all these years and I still try to see them perform every chance I get. At that time, I thought Widespread Panic would be my favorite band forever. But I was in New Orleans, the place where so many great bands come to play. A few months later, during the second semester of my freshman year at Tulane, I became obsessed with another jamband. It was the night after Mardi Gras in 1993. Once again, the club was Tipitina's. And this time the band was — Phish.

THE MUSIC GODS ARE REAL VOL. 1

Even though it happened more than 25 years ago, I remember that night at Tipitina's as if it was yesterday. Phish played their incredible brand of jamband music to a noisy, rowdy, appreciative crowd. Right then and there, Phish became my band, Tipitina's became my church, and live performance music became my new religion. Here is the setlist for Phish's unbelievable performance that evening.

Phish: 3/3/1993 - Tipitina's, New Orleans

I: Rift, Foam, Bouncing Around the Room, Maze, Guelah Papyrus, Paul and Silas>Sample in a Jar, Runaway Jim, Lawn Boy*, Cavern*

II: Axilla, The Curtain>Split Open and Melt, Mound> Mike's Song>I Am Hydrogen>Weekapaug Groove, Glide, My Sweet One, Fast Enough for You, Hold Your Head Up>Terrapin>Hold Your Head Up, The Squirming Coil, Sweet Adeline

E: Fire**

*Carl Gerhard on trumpet
** Jimmy Hendrix Song

Phish had me mesmerized right from the start of the show. They opened with "Rift" and you could tell that they already had the crowd in the palm of their hands. The song "Maze" was intense and suspenseful. The jam was filled with incredible

JONATHAN FINK

moments of building up tension and then euphoric release. The lyrics tell a tale of someone who takes a wrong turn on his life path and as a result, faces failure, shame and the helpless feeling of being lost in a maze unable to find the exit.

I was truly impressed with every aspect of my first Phish performance. I was captivated with how "tight" the band was. I was mesmerized with their precision, raw energy and musicality. I was enthralled with their preparation, intuitiveness and their ability to make musical changes in perfect timing, in sync. I was dancing throughout the entire show and I just could not stop smiling. I may not have known it at that time, but I'm pretty sure now that the Music Gods introduced me to Tipitina's during my freshman year of college so that I would see both Widespread Panic and Phish. Live jamband music would stay in my blood forever.

Trey Anastasio, Phish's extremely talented and charismatic lead singer and guitar player, grew up in a small town in New Jersey, as did both Mihali Savoulidis and Bruce Springsteen. The band was formed in 1983 in Burlington, Vermont, by Anastasio, drummer Jon Fishman, bassist Mike Gordon, and keyboard player Jeff Holdsworth. The group created their name by combining Fishman's nickname, "Fish," with the "phsshh" sound made by a brush on a snare drum. In 1984, while Bruce Springsteen and the E Street Band were living it up on their first world tour, the guys in Phish were playing Grateful Dead cover songs in fraternity houses and small venues in front of small crowds in the Northeast. In 1985, keyboard player Page McConnell joined the band after original member Jeff Holdsworth moved on.

The core of the early song repertoire of Phish was pulled

28

THE MUSIC GODS ARE REAL VOL. 1

from Anastasio's music project at Goddard College, which he called *The Man Who Stepped into Yesterday*. Anastasio submitted the music recording along with a written essay as his senior year thesis. The nine-song rock opera expanded to include eight additional songs and the compilation later became known to fans as "Gamehendge." The band has performed the complete suite of songs that comprise that concept album on only five occasions: in 1988, 1991, 1993 and twice in 1994. A bootleg tape of the original Gamehendge recording began to circulate among the fans and the lore and popularity of Phish began to grow. The good folks at Phish.net explain the rock opera Gamehendge saga the best:

Gamehendge is the mythical land in which *The Man Who Stepped Into Yesterday* takes place. Many Phish songs are part of this story, which is narration interspersed with songs. The story concerns the aging Colonel Forbin, in a suburban town in Long Island, who one day finds a door to another land while walking his faithful dog McGrupp. Stepping through this door, he finds himself in Gamehendge, a land of vast green forests and a huge mountain. Gamehendge is inhabited by the Lizards, who were a simple people who lived in harmony with nature and each other, as taught by the *Helping Friendly Book*, the book containing all knowledge and "the ancient secrets of eternal joy and never-ending splendor." A man named Wilson arrived in Gamehendge and lived among the Lizards, learning all about them. Since they were trusting people, they welcomed him as one of themselves. He took advantage of this, however, and eventually took the *Helping*

JONATHAN FINK

Friendly Book, used it to enslave the Lizards, and hid the book away in a tower. ... At the time that Colonel Forbin enters Gamehendge, when the story as told begins, the lizards are living in bondage to the evil Wilson, and are plotting a revolution.

Like all good fairy tales, the land of Gamehendge has a diverse cast of characters that are described in the story and in the lyrics of its songs. The most important characters are the evil king Wilson and the Lizards, the race of people who inhabit the land. Other colorful characters include McGrupp, Tela, The Famous Mockingbird, The Sloth, Mr. Palmer, The Unit Monster and Icculus, the prophet and author of the *Helping Friendly Book*. Gamehendge is clearly a fairy tale but within the saga are important messages about religion, spirituality and even politics, as told by the brilliant Mr. Anastasio.

I saw Phish again when the band returned to New Orleans in 1994. They were still relatively unknown in the mainstream but were quickly becoming the greatest band you've never heard of. But something amazing happened to Phish at that time. They began to improvise and jam with reckless abandon and their hardcore fans, including me, loved it!

It is hard for me to believe but Phish continues to mature and has gotten even better over time. They blend reggae, jazz, blues, funk, bluegrass and progressive rock and have become well-known and admired for their unbelievably entertaining and unpredictable live shows, for their musical improvisation, for their quirky sense of humor and now more than ever, for their long, extended jams at every performance. Phish, may the Music Gods always be with you!

CHAPTER FIVE

The Grateful Dead

"They're not the best at what they do, they're the only ones
that do what they do."
—Bill Graham

LONG BEFORE THERE WAS PHISH, A TRULY GREAT BAND
paved the way for many jambands to follow. That band was
the Grateful Dead. Their road to the show began in 1965 in
San Francisco, CA, a decade before I was born. Originally
known as the Warlocks, the group quickly changed their name
when they found out that the Velvet Underground, an up and
coming New York City band formed the year before by Lou
Reed, had released a record under the same name. As the story
is told, Jerry Garcia, the band's lead guitar player, took out
a dictionary and randomly pointed his finger at the name —
the Grateful Dead. Perhaps the Music Gods directed Garcia
to select that name since it means "the soul of a dead person,
or his angel, showing gratitude to someone who, as an act of
charity, arranged their burial." A pretty interesting moniker
for a band that would later have their own religious cult-like
following.

JONATHAN FINK

The band blended many musical styles years before there was an E Street Band or Phish. Bluegrass, folk, country, gospel, jazz, psychedelia and space rock were distilled into a unique blend of improvisational rock and roll. the Grateful Dead's flare for experimental and psychedelic music attracted extremely devoted fans and, to a certain extent, a drug culture community. The loyal fans that followed the band and traveled from city to city to see them perform were nicknamed "Deadheads."

The Grateful Dead began their road to the show with almost no radio play. Other much more popular groups, such as the Beatles, the Beach Boys and the Rolling Stones, dominated the mainstream music scene and appealed to a much larger audience. However, with each unique live show, the band gained momentum and succeeded in attracting new, equally devoted followers.

The Grateful Dead thrived on stage and logged more than 2,000 performances on their long road to the show. And as the years went by, the phenomenon that was the Grateful Dead continued to expand. The Deadhead community morphed into a traveling city with its own ecosystem and economy. As the band's tour bus rolled into a new town, the Deadheads would follow and set up their own makeshift village in the stadium parking lot. There you would find food and merchandise vendors and entrepreneurs of all kinds gathering together to share or benefit from the Grateful Dead experience. The fans essentially built a mini, portable shantytown, which eventually earned the nickname "Shakedown Street," after one of the band's popular songs.

In the summer of 1995, after 30 years on his road to the show, Jerry Garcia passed away from a drug overdose and the

32

THE MUSIC GODS ARE REAL VOL. 1

Grateful Dead broke up. Three years later in 1998, the remaining members of the band reunited to tour and perform their Grateful Dead songs calling themselves the Other Ones. In 2003 the band changed its name to the Dead. At the end of the Dead's 2009 tour, bass player Phil Lesh and guitar player Bob Weir formed the band Furthur, which debuted in September of the same year. Other members of the band, Mickey Hart and Bill Kreutzmann, formed the Rhythm Devils and played a summer concert tour.

Since Jerry Garcia's death in 1995, the former members of the Grateful Dead have also pursued solo music careers. Bob Weir & RatDog and Phil Lesh and Friends both performed many concerts and released albums. Mickey Hart and Bill Kreutzmann each released their own individual albums. Hart toured with his world music percussion ensemble Planet Drum as well as the Mickey Hart Band. Kreutzmann led several different bands, including BK3, 7 Walkers (with Papa Mali) and Billy & the Kids. In the fall of 2015, Mickey Hart, Bill Kreutzmann and Bob Weir joined with guitarist John Mayer, keyboardist Jeff Chimenti and bassist Oteil Burbridge to tour in a band they called Dead & Company. And today, the beat of what was the Grateful Dead still goes on.

Ironically, an unknown band that started out playing free concerts in the parks of San Francisco became a multimillion-dollar business empire. In the 1990s, the Grateful Dead earned a total of $285 million in revenue from their concert tours, the second-highest grossing tour during that decade. The Grateful Dead definitely made it on their road to the show, no doubt with the Music Gods showing them the way. The band's merchandise and publishing rights also became

33

JONATHAN FINK

worth millions. The Grateful Dead became a gigantic financial success over the three decades they performed together. I suspect, however, that this was not what the band originally intended. The band was born out of the counter-culture of the 1960s, an era of peace and love, not of war and corporate profits.

As I researched and wrote this chapter about the Grateful Dead and the band's road to fame and fortune, I did have one regret. I never got to see this incredible, groundbreaking group of talented visionaries live in concert. My loss indeed.

CHAPTER SIX

The Patti Rothberg Experience

"Everybody has their day and this one's mine."
—Patti Rothberg

ON THE SUBJECT OF FAME AND FORTUNE AND CORPO-
rate profits, I previously mentioned that my first music internship was in the marketing department of EMI Records, a major
record label. EMI represented some of the biggest names in
the music business at that time and I was looking forward to
learning as much as I could as fast as I could. My plan was
interrupted shortly thereafter, however, when I had a chance
encounter with Alicia Gelernt, the personal manager of a
relatively unknown singer-songwriter named Patti Rothberg.
That's when I joined the music industry counter-culture.

Patti Rothberg grew up in the small, upscale town of
Scarsdale in Westchester County, New York. She started play-
ing piano at the age of three and was writing songs at fifteen.
In high school, Rothberg played in a Rod Stewart cover band.
Unlike John Bell of Widespread Panic and Trey Anastasio of

35

JONATHAN FINK

Phish, who found future bandmates in college, Rothberg graduated college without a band of her own, had an uncertain career direction, and was feeling somewhat lost and without purpose. However, her deep passion for music and art, and her immense talent and creativity, would not permit her to stay idle for long. Patti Rothberg was destined to begin her road to the show and become a success in the music business.

Rothberg began to find her musical style experimenting with new songs at open mic nights whenever and wherever she could. However, faced with the time constraints and limitations of open mic nights and the competition for stage time behind the microphone, she needed to find another outlet. Eventually she found a place where she could play her music and sing her songs for an unlimited audience. Rothberg starting busking for fun underground, in the New York City subway system, playing her guitar and singing her songs between the number 1 and 9 subway lines. Rothberg said she never earned more than eleven dollars in any one day playing for commuters and tourists riding the subways, but she used this time to practice and improve her craft.

Clearly, Rothberg's road to the show was drastically different than the road taken by Bruce Springsteen and the E Street Band, Phish, Widespread Panic, Twiddle, or the Grateful Dead. She was a solo act, a singer-songwriter, just a creative young woman with an acoustic guitar. She had no fan base and had never played a real gig. Yet, the Music Gods had big plans for Rothberg. They connected her with a music manager, Alicia Gelernt, who had many influential contacts and relationships in the music business. The timing for the Rothberg/ Gelernt partnership was divine. Things were percolating in

36

THE MUSIC GODS ARE REAL VOL. 1

the music industry and record labels were eager to get in on the action. John Barry of the *Poughkeepsie Journal* said it best in his article, "Patti Rothberg: Rocker Explores Artistic Side with Paintings" when he wrote:

> She was part of a musical movement. In the wake of the grunge music era, which featured such bands as Nirvana and Pearl Jam, Patti Rothberg was part of a wave of female musicians who brandished a whole lot of attitude and the musical chops to back it up. Rothberg and musicians like Liz Phair, Courtney Love and Ulster County's Tracy Bonham during the 1990s established a signature sound. They showcased individuality with their songs, music and lyrics. And they maintained that individuality as they entrenched themselves in something of a unified front, pushing rock music with a lot of personality beyond boundaries once defined by genres and gender.

Alicia Gelernt successfully created a frenzy and a record label bidding war for Patti Rothberg's talent and potential ensued. Sony Records, Capital Records, Island Records and EMI Records, all major record labels at that time, swarmed in to take a closer look at this new singer-songwriter, hoping first to sign her to their label and second that she would become the next Alanis Morissette or Joan Osborne. EMI Records won the bidding war and embarked on a major campaign to promote Rothberg and make her a commercial success. Rothberg went from playing her guitar and singing her songs for dollar bills in the NYC subway underground to getting a sweet deal, with a signing bonus, with a major record label. With the backing

JONATHAN FINK

of EMI Records, Rothberg got to record her first album at the Electric Lady, the legendary recording studio originally built for the great guitarist Jimi Hendrix.

I began working for Alicia Gelernt as her intern during the summer of 1993 in New York City. I worked endless hours as the studio gopher, running errands and ordering food for Gelernt, Rothberg and her studio band and crew. I usually ordered some food for myself and sat around with all these people involved in the music business, taking in their stories and adventures. Most of the time, however, I just got to hang out, watch, listen and learn. As time went on, I earned Gelernt's trust and she began to value my input and opinions. Shortly thereafter I became her sidekick. I would accompany Gelernt to all of her meetings and often, after a music executive would finish making a comment or offer his opinion, Gelernt would turn to me and ask, "Fink, what do you think?"

Unlike most newcomers to the music scene, including some of the greatest like Springsteen, Phish, and the Grateful Dead, Rothberg's debut album was a success. The album, not surprisingly entitled *Between the 1 and the 9*, reflecting the time Rothberg spent underground in the subway system, went on to sell 250,000 copies in the US and another 200,000 in Europe and Japan. Since Rothberg did not have her own band at the time, she played acoustic, electric and bass guitar on the album. She also did all the vocals and harmonies and even designed and painted her own album cover.

Consistent with her meteoric rise, Rothberg's first single released from *Between the 1 and the 9*, entitled "Inside," was a legit hit. It received regular airplay on radio stations all across the country and the song even got into MTV's rotation on television. After recording the album and the successful release of

THE MUSIC GODS ARE REAL VOL. 1

"Inside," Gelernt worked her magic and had no trouble building a talented band around Rothberg for her shows and the tours expected to follow.

Atypically, Patti Rothberg's road to the show and rise to fame happened very quickly with her EMI record label deal and the successful release of her debut album shortly thereafter. There were no long years of small venues, small crowds and empty seats, only a very brief stint performing underground in the subway system before being discovered. She didn't spend years struggling to create a fan base. Rothberg's career took off from the starting line like a super-fast drag-racing car with the help of her influential manager Alicia Gelernt and, no doubt, the Music Gods.

I rejoined Alicia Gelernt's music management team after graduating college. The timing was perfect. Rothberg was just about to embark on her first tour as the opening act for well-known and very popular singer-songwriter Chris Isaak. Rothberg toured the West Coast with Isaak and I recall thinking at that time that Rothberg's road to the show was paved with gold when she opened for Isaak at the famous Red Rocks Amphitheatre in beautiful Morrison, Colorado.

Rothberg went on to achieve even broader national recognition when she appeared on the *Late Show with David Letterman* and the *Tonight Show with Jay Leno*. Rothberg was even invited to performed a set at the "Jingle Ball" concert, which at the time was held every Christmas season at Madison Square Garden in New York City, perhaps the most well-known music and sports venue in the world. Unlike many artists and bands who work for years before becoming an "overnight sensation," Rothberg became an overnight sensation practically overnight.

JONATHAN FINK

Following up her tour with Chris Isaak and performing on late night national television, Rothberg had the opportunity to go on another tour as the opening act. She had two bands to choose from. One choice was the up-and-coming rock band Matchbox Twenty, with lead singer Rob Thomas at the helm. Matchbox Twenty had a good buzz going after the release of their debut album, *Yourself or Someone Like You*, and their first single off that album, "Long Day," was slowly climbing up the billboard charts. Yet the band was still under the radar of the mainstream music scene. The other band that offered Rothberg an opening tour slot had the number one hit on the radio charts entitled "Standing Outside a Broken Phone Booth with Money in My Hand." I pleaded with Gelernt to convince Rothberg's record label to have her open for Matchbox Twenty, but EMI was convinced that it would be better to tour with a band that at the moment had the most popular song in the country. Unfortunately, that band became a "one-hit wonder," a phrase used in the music business to describe an artist or band that has one big hit and is never heard from again. The "one-hit wonder" that Rothberg toured with was — the Primitive Radio Gods.

CHAPTER SEVEN

The Primitive Radio Gods

"Music is a moral law. It gives soul to the universe, wings to the
mind, flight to the imagination, and charm and gaiety to life
and to everything."

— Plato

THE ROAD TO THE SHOW FOR THE PRIMITIVE RADIO
Gods began in the small town of Oxnard in Southern
California in the late 1980s. Long before the band was known
as the Primitive Radio Gods, the alternative indie rock trio
consisting of lead singer Chris O'Connor, guitarist Jeff Sparks
and drummer Tim Lauterio, were known as the I-Rails. For
years they struggled to find commercial success. After putting
out four indie tapes, none of which generated a buzz, the band
split up. O'Connor, however, would not give up and continued to pursue his dream of making it on the road to the show.

As legend has it, a decade later in 1994 while housecleaning,
O'Connor rediscovered the box of demo tapes he had made
and packed away many years ago. In what has been described

41

as a final act of desperation, O'Connor mailed copies of his dusty old tapes to every major record label he could locate. Shortly thereafter he received a phone call from Jonathan Daniel, a music executive in the New York City office of Fiction Records, a British record label owned by the Universal Music group based in the United Kingdom. One song in particular entitled "Standing Outside a Broken Phone Booth with Money in My Hand" caught Daniel's attention. It was an unusually catchy, piano-driven ballad with a unique hip-hop backbeat. The song also included an alternative rock vibe by heavily sampling B. B. King's "How Blue Can You Get?" Daniel knew he was on to something special and immediately signed the Primitive Radio Gods to a record deal. The song was the lead single from the band's debut album *Rocket* and it was a massive hit.

I learned many things on that Patti Rothberg/Primitive Radio Gods tour. For example, both Rothberg and the Primitive Radio Gods had very limited song catalogues at that time, so they both played almost the exact same setlist every night. Therefore, if a fan caught the show in Philadelphia, there would be no reason to drive down to Washington, DC, to see them again because it would basically be a repeat of the same exact show. Also, not only did both acts play almost identical setlists every night, the Primitive Radio Gods played the songs in the same exact order and the same exact way every time. This approach was in sharp contrast to the live concerts of Bruce Springsteen and Phish, who played different sets at every performance and kept their fans on the edge of their seats wondering which song would be played next.

After a week on the Rothberg/Primitive Radio Gods tour, I wondered if performers ever got bored playing the same songs, the same way, over and over again every night. I suspect some do and some don't. My music business intuition led me to believe that to have long-term success, an artist or band needs to put on a really great, energetic, foot-stomping, sing-along live show every night for their fans and for themselves. To incentivize fans to come out and see more than one show on the tour, performances need to be dynamic and different from night to night. I'm sure the Music Gods would agree.

CHAPTER EIGHT

The Scarecrow Collection

"Gotta love your brother now, gotta love your sister now, try and live
in peace and harmony."
—Scarecrow Collection

MY BOSS, ALICIA GELERNT, WAS ALWAYS LOOKING TO
discover the next great rapper or pop artist, like Patti Rothberg.
However, due to my personal bias, I thought that the next act
she should add to her music management company should be
a jamband. As if directed by the Music Gods, I recall the day I
was in the office digging through a box of demo cassettes looking for a winner when I found a tape with a name of a band
that caught my attention — Scarecrow Collection.

Gerard Fee and his younger brother Joseph were born and
raised in a small town in New Jersey. Both loved music and
each learned to play a musical instrument at an early age.
Gerard learned the guitar, and Joseph took up the drums.
Gerard formed a band with his friends in high school, and
even though Joe was several years younger, he was simply
too talented and mature for his age to not be included in the

THE MUSIC GODS ARE REAL VOL. 1

band. With the approval of their parents, the Fee brothers decked out the basement with Christmas lights and turned the now well-lit lower level of their parents' home into their own rehearsal studio.

I listened to the demo tape of Scarecrow Collection many times over the next several days. I was impressed with what I heard. The more I listened to their music, the more I believed this band had some real potential. In my opinion, Gerard's guitar strumming style, along with Joe's drumming flair, was reminiscent of the Dave Matthews Band, who were very popular at that time. The band also included a harmonica and mandolin player which gave them a little bit of a bluegrass feel. Shortly thereafter, I spoke with Alicia about Scarecrow Collection and asked if I could follow up on my discovery. Like every successful music manager with a nose for talent, she told me to go for it, and I did.

I contacted the band and explained who I was and why I was getting in touch with them. They were excited to be approached by a reputable New York City music management company and invited me to hear them perform. I took the subway to 34th Street and transferred to the PATH train out to the suburbs of New Jersey. Gerard picked me up at their local train station stop in the family minivan, which eventually evolved into the band's tour bus. After formal introductions, we headed to the Fee family home.

Foregoing the full house tour, down the stairs we went to their music den in the basement of their parents' house. And that's where I thought I'd found music heaven. That night the band auditioned all their songs from the demo tape, including two of their favorites, "When the World Blows Up" and

JONATHAN FINK

"Hill." It was like a private concert just for me and one of the highlights of the evening was that the band found their way into a jam with each song they played. To my very pleasant surprise, Scarecrow Collection was a jamband!

I could tell right away that the Scarecrow Collection had raw talent and great chemistry. It was obvious that these high school buddies loved playing together and I enjoyed every minute listening to them play. It was clearly too early to know whether any of them possessed extraordinary talent and the charisma necessary to succeed in the very competitive music business, except possibly for the wonderkid drummer Joey, who was clearly talented beyond his years. Yet, they played really well together and sounded great. It was also obvious to me that like all great athletes, entertainers and musicians, Scarecrow Collection took every opportunity to practice, practice, practice and it paid off.

During the breaks of their showcase performance, the band members and I sat on the closed-in Fee family porch. We talked about our favorite bands and the music we gravitated to. I was very surprised that they had never heard of Phish and were unfamiliar with their music. I urged them to listen to Phish. I also encouraged them to listen to Strangefolk, an up-and-coming jamband from Vermont, because in my opinion that band had many similarities to Scarecrow Collection and they really knew how to jam. My intention was not for Scarecrow Collection to copy these bands but to learn from them and expand their musical and jamband capabilities.

For the next several weeks, I traveled by train to New Jersey to nurture my relationship with Scarecrow Collection. I truly enjoyed watching them rehearse and was pleased to see that

THE MUSIC GODS ARE REAL VOL. 1

they continued to improve and add material to their repertoire. During breaks on the porch, I started to get to know the
members in the band a lot better. They were all such good-na-
tured kids and it became clear to me that they possessed the
desire and passion to succeed. I loved their comradery and the
easy way they related to one another. And I truly appreciated
how grateful they were that I had taken an interest in them and
wanted to help them.

I knew this was the kind of band I wanted to manage. Don't
get me wrong, I loved working with Patti Rothberg. But at the
same time, I wanted to help Alicia expand her music management company and I saw Scarecrow Collection as a big opportunity for a "jamband business model." I felt certain that night
that I would manage a jamband and have a long career in the
music business.

After weeks of preparation and rehearsals, I felt Scarecrow
Collection was ready for the next step. I booked their first
professional gig at the Crossroads on the Upper East Side in
New York City. I could tell the band was nervous and on edge
before they went on stage, and they played for an essentially
empty room that night. But they seemed thrilled with the experience. Here they were, a group of high school buddies from
the suburbs of New Jersey, playing a set in New York City!
For me, watching from the floor in front of the stage, their
performance was exciting and gratifying. I had booked my
first show for my first band, and in New York City no less. I
was proud of what I had accomplished.

Thereafter, I was successful in booking gigs for Scarecrow
Collection at many venues in NYC and New Jersey, including
the famous Bottom Line in Greenwich Village, the hot spot

47

JONATHAN FINK

where Bruce Springsteen performed his famous five-night, ten-show run. At that point in time, I was sure music management was my future. What I didn't know at the time was that the Music Gods had other plans for me.

There were some bumps on the road for the Scarecrow Collection and for me. One time, I booked the band into a well-known venue in Greenwich Village called The Lion's Den. As a pre-condition, the owner requested a guarantee that a certain number of people would attend the show. I was a young, confident kid just out of college so I foolishly agreed, fully expecting a big crowd that night. When we could not deliver enough fans to meet the guarantee, the owner was very angry at the world, mostly with me. He aggressively confronted me and just when he was about to pick me up and throw me into a wall, in walked my boss, Alicia, to check in with me and watch the Scarecrow performance. Like a movie superhero arriving on the scene unexpectedly to save the day, Alicia rescued me that night by talking to the owner and extricating me out of a very unpleasant and contentious situation. Notwithstanding, after the show the club owner told me that he would never let Scarecrow Collection play there ever again, nor would he let me book any other band there in the future. I was devasted.

Despite that one awkward moment with the angry club owner, I continued to represent Scarecrow Collection and my time helping the band was a truly enjoyable and rewarding experience. In fact, it was amazing. I remember clearly the last gig I booked for the band before I left my job with Gelernt Music Management. It was in Woodstock, NY. It was the Scarecrow Collection's first road trip and mine as well.

THE MUSIC GODS ARE REAL VOL. 1

Unfortunately, just as the band began its road to the show, the wheels began to slowly fall off the Fee family minivan. First the harmonica player was ousted from the band and was eventually replaced with a lead guitar player. While the harmonica player was no John Popper, it was clear that some of the band's special chemistry was lost after he left. Despite some success a decade later, I don't think Scarecrow Collection was ever the same thereafter.

Shortly after I helped Scarecrow Collection get started on their road to the show, I decided to leave the music business to pursue other adventures. These adventures included two years at the Bloch School of Business in Kansas City to earn my MBA, 13 years as a financial advisor with Morgan Stanley in New York and Leawood, and starting Satya Investment Management, my own investment firm. The band, however, stayed together and carried on without me.

Although no longer in the music business, I continued to follow Scarecrow Collection. Despite some struggles, the band did bring its unique brand of roots-oriented folk rock to the masses and played over 300 shows from 2001 to 2007. They got their first real taste of the show in 2006 when they were invited to play at the 11th Annual Gathering of the Vibes Music Festival at Seaside Park in Bridgeport, Connecticut, an experience originally conceived to celebrate the life of Grateful Dead lead guitarist Jerry Garcia and bring music lovers together for a long weekend of spiritual renewal.

It was after the Gathering of the Vibes Music Festival in 2007 that the Scarecrow Collection noticed that something was missing when they jammed. It took some time and some serious soul searching for them to conclude that they were

49

JONATHAN FINK

no longer a real jamband. In an interview for an article entitled "Homegrown Band Scarecrow Collection Developing an Identity of its Own," guitarist Nick Setteducato said, "We've started to realize that you don't have to force the jam." Gerard Fee added, "For a long time, there would be these 10-minute jams, 15-minute jams in the middle of the song, but for the past year or two, we've tried to focus on how the song as a whole sounds. And it's cool, because we're starting to sound like ourselves, rather than trying to sound like other bands." With this change, it seemed that the band's signature sound was gone, and to make matters worse in my opinion, they no longer jammed like they used to.

The new lineup struggled to find chemistry and their groove without the jams, and their live shows failed to gain a devoted following of fans. Scarecrow Collection ground on for a few more years, but the magic that I witnessed under those Christmas lights in 1998 in the basement of the Fee family home was now a distant memory. This proved to me that the Music Gods can be fickle and that not all stories about bands on the music road to the show have happy endings.

CHAPTER NINE

The Black Crowes

"I think that some of the best Crowes stuff we did had that spontaneous vibe. That's something that's always interested me in music."

—Chris Robinson

SCARECROW COLLECTION WAS NOT THE ONLY BAND I crossed paths with during my short tenure in the music management business. I also intersected with the Black Crowes, a far more well-known band that was already pretty far along on their road to the show when we met. While the Black Crowes were on a different and much more successful path than Scarecrow Collection, their tale has, at least for now, a somewhat unhappy ending.

This was another instance where the Music Gods had a plan for me. Long before I actually met the Black Crowes, when I accompanied Patti Rothberg as the band's opening act when they toured throughout Europe, a Black Crowes poster hung on my bedroom wall. They were one of my favorite bands as a teenager.

The Black Crowes were formed by brothers Chris and Rich Robinson, who grew up in Marietta, Georgia, a lovely

JONATHAN FINK

suburb about 25 miles northwest of Atlanta. In 1984, when Bruce Springsteen and the E Street Band were embarking on their worldwide *Born in the U.S.A.* Tour, the Robinson brothers were attending Walton High School and putting their first band together. They named that band Mr. Crowe's Garden after a children's book entitled *Johnny Crow's Garden*. They developed their sound which morphed into a unique blend of psychedelic blues and southern rock 'n' roll, sort of like blending the Rolling Stones with the Allman Brothers Band. After adding drummer Steve Gorman to the band, the group changed their name to the Black Crowes.

The Black Crowes' road to the show began in earnest after one of their demo tapes led to a record deal. Three years later in 1990, their first album, *Shake Your Money Maker*, was a big commercial success. The album achieved multi-platinum status and eventually sold more than five million copies. With each single, the Black Crowes received more play on radio and air time on MTV. Ironically, their cover of soul and rhythm and blues legend Otis Redding's "Hard to Handle" became the band's biggest hit. This album became a classic with so many great songs including "Jealous Again," "Twice as Hard, "She Talks to Angels," "Sister Luck" and "Seeing Things." Shortly thereafter, when the Black Crowes hit the road to promote their debut album, they were a straight up rock and roll band, not a jamband.

On their first tour, the Black Crowes opened for ZZ Top, the well-known trio from Houston, Texas, famous for their super long beards and southern rock style, who already had more than a decade of success in the music business. The group moved even further away from the jamband music scene on

52

THE MUSIC GODS ARE REAL VOL. 1

their next tour, when they opened the *Monsters of Rock Tour* in Europe which included heavy metal bands Metallica, AC/ DC, Mötley Crüe and Queensrÿche. By sharing the stage with these extremely popular heavy metal bands, it was clear that the Black Crowes were on the fast track to stardom.

After the release of *Shake Your Money Maker*, which I loved, and the tour that followed, the band replaced their lead guitar player Jeff Cease with Marc Ford. Perhaps it was Ford's influence on the band or just coincidence, but the Black Crowes' second album, *The Southern Harmony and Musical Companion*, was breathtaking. It was like a religious experience for me. The album was well produced. The songs and lyrics were great. The infusion of keyboard and organ added a new element to the band's sound. The new album had Ford's enhanced lead guitar sound layered on top of Rich Robinson's rhythm guitar playing. The album also added a group of soul singers to back up and harmonize with Chris Robinson. The Black Crowes had successfully transformed themselves between their first and second albums, and I, like their growing fan base, was pleased with the result.

The Southern Harmony and Musical Companion debuted at #1 on the *Billboard* charts and was another commercial success. I recall being so impressed, almost in awe, as I listened to each song for the very first time. "Remedy," "Sting Me," "Thorn in My Pride" and "Hotel Illness" all charted on *Billboard*. It was crystal clear that this band's first album was no fluke. I knew then that they would be around for years to come.

Looking back now, I remember in high school even more clearly listening to the back half of the *Southern Harmony* album for the first time and being so impressed. Usually,

53

JONATHAN FINK

producers place a band's best songs at the front of an album. Well, perhaps this Black Crowes' album simply had no weaknesses. While I thought the songs on the front side of the album were fantastic, my favorite songs were actually on the second side of the album. The gritty, hard rocking, bluesy songs "Black Moon Creeping," "No Speak No Slave" and "My Morning Song" were simply next level. Chris Robinson's vocals danced in my ears, as did the female backup singers who chimed in during the chorus of each song. The lyrics really moved me as well. I felt as if Chris Robinson was singing like a preacher spreading the gospel and dishing out some hard truths about life.

Something else felt different to me on this album. In the epic rock classic "My Morning Song," the band broke the song down in the middle of the track and built up to a nice "jam" on their way to the song's final chorus. Perhaps that little jam was a foreshadowing of things to come for the Black Crowes in the future. *Southern Harmony* had added lots of keyboard and organ play to the music. So, when the band got back on the road to the show to promote the album's release, they added the very talented keyboard player Eddie Harsch to the mix. As their *High as the Moon Tour* began, it was clear that the Black Crowes were no longer just a straight up rock and roll band. On this tour, they started to jam.

I saw the Black Crowes play at the Jones Beach Theater on Long Island when they headlined the jamband-oriented *H.O.R.D.E. Tour*. After the band played a fabulous 30-minute version of "Thorn in My Pride," I was beaming with pride that one of my favorite rock bands since high school had become one of the best jambands around. I wonder if the Music Gods played a role in the band's transformation.

54

THE MUSIC GODS ARE REAL VOL. 1

The Black Crowes' success continued with the release of two more terrific albums, *Amorica* and *Three Snakes and One Charm*. With four great albums' worth of material, the band now had the flexibility to change their live performance setlists from night to night and keep their growing fan base on the edge of their seats, like Bruce Springsteen did.

While working closely with Patti Rothberg during my Gelernt Music Management days, I had the privilege of traveling with Patti as she toured with the Black Crowes throughout Europe as their opening act. Since Rothberg was a pop-rock act, she may not have been the best fit as an opening act for a jamband like the Black Crowes. But for me, touring with Patti Rothberg and the Black Crowes across Europe was a dream come true.

The Black Crowes had to be excited when they were asked to join the *Furthur Festival Tour* during the summer of 1997. The lineup for the *Furthur Festival* featured the Black Crowes, moe., Sherri Jackson, Bruce Hornsby, Jorma Kaukonen & Michael Falzarano, Arlo Guthrie, RatDog, Mickey Hart & Planet Drum and Robert Hunter. At the end of every show, all of the performers would come on stage for an all-star jam. What better way for Chris and Rich Robinson to learn the ways of the jamband than jamming night after night with Bob Weir and Mickey Hart of the Grateful Dead.

The Black Crowes had made it on their road to the show. Unfortunately, Chris and Rich Robinson apparently had a challenging long-term "love-hate" relationship and infighting between the brothers took its toll on the band. Eventually, this caused the band to break up. The group reunited a few years later, but the reunion did not last long as old problems with the Robinson brothers reemerged.

JONATHAN FINK

In my opinion, it's a shame that the Black Crowes broke up. They were a great band. Unlike so many talented bands that do not make it on their road to the show, the Black Crowes had made it all the way. Perhaps further down this highway of life, the Music Gods will conspire to reunite the Robinson brothers once again.

CHAPTER TEN

The Year Phish Became Phish

"Set the gearshift for the high gear of your soul, you've got to run like an antelope out of control."

— Phish

I HAVE LONG FELT THAT 1994 WAS A TRANSFORMA-tional year for Phish. After forming in 1983 and touring the country relentlessly from 1988 through 1993, the Phish scene felt like a boiling pot of water that was ready to blow sky high. While researching for this project, I discovered an entire book dedicated to the 1994 Phish tour. It turns out that I was not the only one that felt the same way about Phish at this time.

In his book entitled *This Has All Been Wonderful*, author David Steinberg gives a show-by-show review of his summer traveling the country with Phish in 1994. Steinberg notes that prior to this time the band didn't really jam on a regular basis. He explains that Phish was still playing tiny clubs and since the band was still sufficiently unknown, they would hang out with the fans before and after shows. Steinberg says that in those early days before 1994, the band did not jam very much even though they played with a ferocious energy.

I was introduced to Phish by my dear friend Eric Milano

when we both were counselors at Camp Schodack during the summer of 1991. With his boombox in hand, he had me listen to a cassette tape of his new favorite band. The first Phish song he played for me was "Reba." The lyrics were a little silly but the song was catchy, funny and witty. The chorus of the song had a really good hook, "Bag it, tag it, sell it to the butcher in the store." However, the song changed dramatically at around the two minute and thirty-five second mark. At this part of the song, Phish left the traditional song format that had the silly lyrics and clever chorus and began the most incredible pre-arranged musical instrumental. I had never heard anything like this Phish song before and I loved it.

The first compact disc I purchased at Tulane's off-campus music store, The Mushroom, was the Phish album *Junta*. I had that CD on repeat in my freshman dorm. Perhaps I began manifesting Phish into my life at that time because a few months later, I learned that Phish was scheduled to play a show at Tipitina's. I knew I had to go and did.

A year later, during my sophomore year, Phish returned to New Orleans and performed on Tulane's campus at McAlister Auditorium. The Music Gods were now just showing off. The show was particularly memorable for me because on the way to the show, walking through Tulane's campus passing by PJ's Coffee shop at the University Center quad, I realized that I had lost my ticket. But the Music Gods came to my rescue. When I ran back and retraced my steps, I luckily found my ticket on the ground. It felt like a ticket miracle.

That night at McAlister Auditorium, I got to hear my first songs from Gamehendge performed live and in person. As I watched and listened to Phish play a part of the Gamehendge saga, I was in awe, as was everyone else in the audience. It was

THE MUSIC GODS ARE REAL VOL. 1

extraordinary to watch Phish turn my college campus into a psychedelic frenzy that night. It was simply amazing. I also felt a sense of pride that my favorite band was playing at my school. It does not get much better than that. Here is the setlist from that incredible performance.

Phish: 10/14/94 McAlister Auditorium - Tulane University, New Orleans, LA

I: Buried Alive > Sample in a Jar > Divided Sky, The Horse > Silent in the Morning, Punch You in the Eye, Bathtub Gin, Sweet Adeline, Rift, Colonel Forbin's Ascent > Fly Famous Mockingbird, Julius

II: The Curtain > Tweezer > Lifeboy, Guyute, Chalk Dust Torture, Nellie Kane (1), Beaumont Rag (1), Foreplay/Long Time (1), The Squirming Coil, Tweezer Reprise

E: Ya Mar (2), Cavern

1. Acoustic
2. Michael Ray on trumpet and shaker and Carl Gerhard on trumpet.

Earlier in the year, Phish released the album *Hoist*, so their 1994 tour was filled with lots of new songs. The band also began to cater to their growing community of loyal fans known as "Phishheads." For example, the band introduced a tickets-by-mail program which enabled tapers and traveling fans to use a convenient mail order system to obtain tickets for shows. The band also made their tour more convenient for their traveling fans by scheduling more multi-night stands such as their three-night-run at the Beacon Theatre on the Upper West Side of New York City.

Musically speaking, Phish also took their craft to the next level in 1994. The band played with such spontaneity that anything became possible during a show. For example, Phish was playing a concert at the Eagles Ballroom in Milwaukee, Wisconsin, on the night that famous ex-football player O.J. Simpson became a person of interest in a murder investigation. As O.J. tried to escape police officers by driving on the highway in his white Ford Bronco, the Phish concert played on. The nation literally came to a standstill as the news interrupted all television programming to follow the police pursuit down the Los Angeles Freeway. Everyone in the country dropped what they were doing to watch the high-speed chase live on television. Phish kept performing their show, but they knew what was happening on TV, so they incorporated plenty of O.J. teases riddled throughout this famous performance. That concert became known as the infamous "O.J. Show."

Phish started the O.J. teases during the perfectly placed opening song, "Runaway Jim." Trey dedicated the song to "Orenthal James Simpson." Later, during "Also Sprach Zarathustra (2001)", the band started screaming "O.J.!" at various points in the song. The second set included more teases about O.J. especially during "My Poor Heart," "Mike's Song," "Simple," and "Harpua." During the "Mike's Song" jam, Phish played the *Mission: Impossible* theme song. Jon Fishman throughout the jam kept yelling, "Run O.J. Run!" While it was not really a laughing matter, that Phish show was hilarious.

THE MUSIC GODS ARE REAL VOL. 1

Phish: 6/17/94 - Eagles Ballroom, Milwaukee, WI

I: Runaway Jim (1), Foam, Glide, Split Open and Melt, If I Could, Punch You in the Eye > Bathtub Gin, Scent of a Mule, Cavern

II: Also Sprach Zarathustra (1) > Sample in a Jar, Poor Heart (1) > Mike's Song (1) -> Simple (1) -> Mike's Song > I Am Hydrogen > Weekapaug Groove, Harpua -> Kung -> Harpua (1), Sparkle > Big Ball Jam > Julius > Frankenstein

E: Sleeping Monkey > Rocky Top
1.O.J. Reference

A few months after playing the legendary "O.J. Show," Phish surprised their fans by playing a full "Gamehendge show." By the fall of 1994, Phish was playing with more improvisation and spontaneity than ever, but now they were also using their setlists as a way to express their musical creativity.

On Halloween night in 1994, Phish performed their first "musical costume," a three-set concert with the middle set dedicated to only cover songs of a particular band. Phish does not cover just one song, they cover an entire album! For their first musical costume ever, shown below, Phish boldly covered the Beatles' *White Album*.

Phish: 10/31/94 - Glens Falls Civic Center, Glens Falls, NY

I: Frankenstein, Sparkle > Simple > Divided Sky, Harpua ->

The Vibration of Life -> Harpua, Julius > The Horse >
Silent in the Morning > Reba, Golgi Apparatus

II: Back in the U.S.S.R.> Dear Prudence, Glass Onion>
Ob-La-Di, Ob-La-Da, Wild Honey Pie, The Continuing Story
of Bungalow Bill, While My Guitar Gently Weeps, Happiness
Is a Warm Gun, Martha My Dear, I'm So Tired, Blackbird,
Piggies, Rocky Raccoon > Don't Pass Me By, Why Don't We
Do It in the Road?, I Will, Julia, Birthday, Yer Blues, Mother
Nature's Son, Everybody's Got Something to Hide Except
Me and My Monkey, Sexy Sadie, Helter Skelter, Long, Long,
Long, Revolution 1, Honey Pie, Savoy Truffle, Cry Baby
Cry -> Revolution 9

III: David Bowie, Bouncing Around the Room, Slave to the
Traffic Light > Rift > Sleeping Monkey > Poor Heart, Run
Like an Antelope

E: Amazing Grace, Costume Contest, The Squirming Coil

Before the 1994 calendar year ended, Phish sold out Madison
Square Garden and Boston Garden. This was the culmination
of a remarkable ascent for a band that had slowly been grinding its way on its road to the show for a decade. It was as if the
band reached an inflection point that year, like the hundredth
monkey analogy. By the end of 1994, it was clear that Phish
had finally made it on their road to the show.

CHAPTER ELEVEN

The Clifford Ball

"The passion that sparked me one terrible night and shocked and
persuaded my soul to ignite."

— Phish

CLEARLY, 1994 WAS THE BREAKTHROUGH YEAR FOR
Phish. However, two years later in 1996, the band became a
music titan. In fact, Phish was so popular and successful, the
band boldly created and hosted its very own music festival
called *The Clifford Ball*.

That summer more than 70,000 fans traveled to the former
Plattsburg Air Force Base in upstate New York for the first
music festival of its kind. I was one of those pioneering
Phishheads who attended that festival. The event was named
after a man who held special events for aviators, such as
Amelia Earhart, at the former aviation field. Not surprisingly,
his name was — Clifford Ball.

Walking inside the festival grounds, I felt like I had stepped
into a fairy tale land inside a different dimension of space and

JONATHAN FINK

time, just like Colonel Forbin in the land of Gamehendge. It was wonderful. I recall walking by jugglers, art installations and even a classical violin quartet. There were movies playing on big screens in the camping area. A full village reminiscent of the Deadheads' Shakedown Street was built on a hill. There was even a general store and a Ben and Jerry's stand offering free ice cream. The only flavor served, of course, was Phish Food, the flavor named after the band. The setlist Phish performed that day was remarkable and memorable.

Phish: 8/16/96 - *The Clifford Ball*, Plattsburgh, NY

I: Chalk Dust Torture, Bathtub Gin, Ya Mar, AC/DC Bag > Esther > Divided Sky, Halley's Comet > David Bowie

II: Split Open and Melt, Sparkle > Free, The Squirming Coil, Waste, Talk, Train Song, Strange Design, Hello My Baby, Mike's Song -> Simple -> Contact > Weekapaug Groove

III: Makisupa Policeman > Also Sprach Zarathustra > Down with Disease -> NICU, Life on Mars? > Harry Hood -> Jam
Encore: Amazing Grace

The Clifford Ball was a smashing success and made headline news in the mainstream media, including a piece in *Rolling Stone* magazine. Phish was finally getting music industry recognition and now the band's road to the show was on a superhighway.

CHAPTER TWELVE

The Year Phish Broke Up

"Surrender to the flow."
— Phish

THE FIRST WARNING SIGN CAME IN 2000 WHEN PHISH announced that they were going on a "hiatus." It lasted 815 days, from October 7, 2000 to December 31, 2002. When the band reunited and returned to the stage, something was missing. The chemistry was not the same. The band was not as tight as they used to be and the jams were less often and not as dynamic as they were back in the good old days of 1994. Sometime thereafter in 2004, word came that Phish was not just taking another break, they were breaking up for good.

The initial reasons given for the breakup included a desire for the band members to spend more time with family, concerns about the organization becoming a burden, the pressure of expectations, and the desire to avoid becoming a nostalgia act. However, fans later learned that the real reason for the breakup was that Trey Anastasio had developed a drug problem and he needed time away from the band and touring to get clean and sober. Like Scarecrow Collection, the

65

JONATHAN FINK

Black Crowes and the Grateful Dead, Phish's road to the show appeared to be over sooner than expected. The entire Phish community was emotionally crushed, including me. After all, for many Phish fans, the band and its music had become a way of life, almost like being part of an organized religion.

Writer Richard Lei explained how Phish fans viewed the band and its music from a very spiritual perspective in his 1994 *Washington Post* article "The Hottest Band the World Has Never Heard." Lei wrote:

All Phish fans — be they suburban teeny-boppers or erudite college students, grimy homeless hippies or married-with-kids professionals — talk about the uplifting "vibe" of the band's live performances, the inexplicable "connection" they feel with the musicians, though they rarely address the crowd. Some fans cite the spiritual charge they get from a Phish concert, although the band itself espouses no religious mission or message. At best, the members of Phish offer awkward explanations for their cult like following. "It's an intangible energy," attempts Trey Anastasio, the shaggy red-haired guitarist... "It's a spiritual phenomenon, not just entertainment," argues professor Rebecca Adams, a sociologist at the University of North Carolina. "But it's not a belief in musicians as deities. It's a belief in the power of music to create community.

With Phish gone from the jamband music scene in 2004, a new vacuum was created that needed to be filled for the first time since Jerry Garcia had passed away in 1995. Enter Mihali Savoulidis, Ryan Dempsey, and their band — Twiddle.

CHAPTER THIRTEEN

The Great Gatsby

"We're like licorice. Not everybody likes licorice, but the people who like licorice really like licorice."
— Jerry Garcia

MIHALI SAVOULIDIS ALWAYS KNEW THAT ONE DAY HE would go to college, join a band and pursue his music career full time. Following in the footsteps of jamband legend Trey Anastasio from Phish, Mihali made his way up to Vermont to attend college. During Anastasio's freshman year, he had met Jon Fishman, who became Phish's co-founder and drummer. As Mihali left his dorm room for the first day of orientation at Castleton University, he went looking for his own Jon Fishman. Mihali met Ryan Dempsey for the first time sitting right next to him that day. They became instant friends and were soon writing songs together in their dorm rooms. Mihali and Ryan found the name of their new band the same way that Jerry Garcia did for the Grateful Dead. They randomly pointed a finger in the dictionary and landed on Twiddle.

The second song Mihali and Ryan wrote together was "Gatsby the Great," a song about a duck that Ryan tried to

JONATHAN FINK

train as his pet. The song, which became their first "jam vehicle," had a catchy melody and the lyrics told a cute story about the duck. Most importantly, helped by Ryan's background in classical music theory, Mihali and Ryan wrote a beautiful jam-oriented musical composition with several musical sections embedded into the song. With practice and creativity, Twiddle quickly discovered that they could play a part of the composed piece of the song, move into an improvisational jam, and then find their way back into another section of the song later on. Thus, right from the start, Twiddle's "reggae-jam" musical style was accompanied with improvisation jamming.

Mihali and Ryan realized soon thereafter that they needed more members to complete their band. First, they found a talented drummer in Brook Jordan. Then they found their perfect bass guitar player in Zdenek Gubb, who was just 17 years old at the time and still in high school. Gubb was already a fan of Twiddle and would frequently attend their shows. When the age limit at certain venues prevented Gubb from attending some shows, he would hang out with friends near the back door of the venue so he could listen.

As the story goes, Gubb discovered his love for the bass guitar when his older brother had him listen to the band Primus. The sounds coming from Les Claypool's bass guitar had Gubb in awe. With this as background, Gubb brought his funky base sound to Twiddle. I have learned that drum and bass are critical parts of a good jamband. The drummer actually controls the direction and pace of a jam. While the guitar and keyboard players usually get all the credit, the bass and drums keep the jams grooving on.

Once joining Twiddle, Gubb and Jordan quickly mastered the improvisational art of jamming known as "tension and

THE MUSIC GODS ARE REAL VOL. 1

release." Tension is produced through reiteration and an increase in dynamic level to create the eventual payoff of euphoric sonic bliss once the "tension" in the jam is "released." In the months that followed, the band wrote some great songs to accompany their ever-improving jamming. In the early days, Twiddle's most popular songs were about imaginative characters such as Carter Candlestick, Hattibagen McRat, Cabbage Face, Tiberius, the Jamflowman and Frankenfoote. This was similar to Phish, who began their rise to popularity with songs about make believe characters in the land of Gamehendge.

Like Bruce Springsteen and Phish had done in their early years, Twiddle toured as much as possible to attract attention and a fan base. In 2005 the band played their first 3 shows, all local. By 2008, the band branched out to a wider demographic, including New York, Connecticut, Massachusetts, Maine and even Montreal, Canada. In 2009, however, rather than continuing to increase their workload, the band slowed down and played just 37 shows.

While Twiddle continued to improve as a band, the jamband community at large was hardly taking notice. The band was still playing to small crowds in small clubs. The band members were starting to lose faith on their road to the show. Perhaps the reason Twiddle felt it had reached a plateau at this time was because many of the band's fans flocked back to Phish when the group reunited once again and returned to touring. Also, the Grateful Dead reincarnated as several different bands, further saturating the market in the jamband scene. Finally, other talented jambands started to make their mark on the jamband scene. Jambands like the String Cheese Incident, the Disco Biscuits, moe., and Umphrey's McGee were all winning over former Phish fans. For Mihali, Ryan,

JONATHAN FINK

Jordan and Gubb, it began to feel like they were in stuck in a traffic jam on the busy highway. It was as if Twiddle was experiencing a midlife crisis.

In some ways I could relate to what Twiddle was going through. At the age of 38, I experienced my own midlife crisis. I had been a successful financial advisor at Morgan Stanley for many years. However, after moving from New York to Kansas City, followed by a severe stock market reversal, I lost many of my clients to other financial firms. I began a downward emotional spiral that led to negative thinking. My thoughts were creating my reality. The more negative I became about the world and my client relationships, the worse my reality seemed to be, and more of my clients sought advice elsewhere.

Even during those dark days, I still listened to music for enjoyment and support. Looking back now, I can see a direct correlation between my emotions at different times in my life and the music that I listened to at the same time. During my angriest days, I often listened to the punk rock band Sum 41. During my saddest days, I listened to Mumford & Sons. As my yoga and meditation practice began to take hold, I listened to Michael Franti, MC Yogi and Trevor Hall. Then, as my happiness, comfort and confidence slowly increased, I started listening to Bruce Springsteen and the E Street Band again. At least once a day, while driving in the car or taking my dogs Charlie and Buddy for a walk, I would listen to the Bruce Springsteen classic — The Promised Land.

CHAPTER FOURTEEN

The Promised Land

*"Blow away the dreams that tear you apart.
Blow away the dreams that break your heart.
Blow away the lies that leave you nothing
but lost and brokenhearted."*
— Bruce Springsteen

I TRULY BELIEVE THAT THE MUSIC YOU CHOOSE TO listen to becomes the soundtrack of your life. Whether listening while driving in your car, on your headphones while on a jog, or in-person at a concert of your favorite band, the music you are hearing is consciously and subconsciously impacting your emotions. Your emotions affect your thoughts, and your thoughts create your reality. To a great extent, the music you listen to will shape your outlook on life and may even determine your level of happiness.

Prior to the stock market reversal, my success as a financial advisor at the investment firm Morgan Stanley was at an all-time high. Unfortunately, my arrogance from years of consistently "beating the market" was also at an all-time high. Admittedly, my obsession with the world's problems

JONATHAN FINK

and conspiracy theories was also at an all-time high. I was like a Boeing 747 flying through the sky on cruise control and I was too confident or blind to see that my plane's fuel tank was running on empty. It was only a matter of time before my investment career success came crashing down just like the stock market. My arrogance and negative thinking had upset the Investment Gods and it was time for me to pay back the karmic debts that I had created.

Two years after my family moved from New York to Kansas City, an up-and-coming folk-rock band from London, England, played a club in Kansas City called "recordBar." That band was Mumford & Sons. It may have taken years for Mumford & Sons to get going on their road to the show in their native land, but in the United States, they became one of the most popular bands around in just a few short years. For example, when Mumford & Sons first performed in Kansas City, they did so in front of only 400 people at recordBar, just a block away from the Sprint Center. When the band returned to Kansas City a year later, they were playing the city market in front of 10,000 screaming fans.

I saw my first Mumford & Sons show with my wife Reggie in Bonner Springs, Kansas, at the Sandstone Amphitheater, now known as the Providence Medical Center Amphitheater. The band played to a sold-out crowd of devotees that seemed to know every word of every song lead singer Marcus Mumford sang. The next time Mumford & Sons played Kansas City, I saw the band perform to another sold-out crowd, this time at the Sprint Center, the biggest indoor venue in Kansas City with almost 20,000 seats.

While they are not a jamband, I fell in love with Mumford

72

& Sons, their music and their orchestration. The band had a unique sound, a fusion of bluegrass, folk, country and rock. Many of their songs had an eerie feel to them and often built up momentum as the song went on. At the end of many of their songs, it felt as if the band was playing together like a full orchestra of bluegrass sonic blessedness. When they performed live, the band carried themselves with the energy and power of a traditional rock band. Marcus Mumford's vocals were unique and he always sang with such emotion, the audience could almost feel his emotional pain. Many of the band's songs were about love, loss, suffering and regret.

As Mumford & Sons' sad and deeply emotional songs were gaining popularity around the world, they were also gaining critics. Interestingly, while researching for this book, I found several articles written about how sad and depressing the band's songs were. A blog post from the website *The Zoo* entitled "The Mumford Depressing Scale" ranks twenty of their songs from most depressing to least depressing. I also found an article entitled "Give Me the Feels: Mumford & Sons: Deep Cutting Mumford & Sons Songs Just to Enhance Those Sad, Sad Feels" penned by writer Cody Deitz. In fact, their sad songs were impacting the band members themselves. In a BBC article entitled "Mumford & Sons on Death, Depression and Divorce," lead singer Marcus Mumford was quoted as saying, "I've definitely been closer to death in the last year than I've ever been."

I stayed in the dark energy of the songs of Mumford & Sons for many months, and I had a hard time breaking free. It was almost as if their dark music kept me in a low vibrational state of being. This situation continued into 2012, when the band released a live album, recorded in Morrison, Colorado, at the famous Red Rocks Amphitheatre, entitled *The Road to Red Rocks*. This album was filled with typical Mumford and Sons negativity. The band also filmed a documentary of the live performance and gave the film the same title, *The Road to Red Rocks*.

The Music Gods know I have a soft spot for live music and I have always loved live albums like Bob Dylan's *Bootleg Series*. It is live on stage that you find out just how good a band really is. Mumford & Sons' live album at Red Rocks was terrific. The band's musicianship was outstanding and their songs grew on me even more. But it never occurred to me at the time that *The Road to Red Rocks* was keeping me in negative thought patterns and also a low vibrational state of being. Mumford & Sons' music was part of my regular rotation. Consciously and subconsciously, their songs about guilt, depression and heartbreak were feeding into my mind and my soul. To make matters worse, my sad and depressing thoughts were now clearly manifesting into my reality, leading me further down my midlife crisis road.

Long before there was Mumford & Sons or their *The Road to Red Rocks* live album, I had been fascinated with the Red Rocks Amphitheatre. Perhaps it was that U2 music video "Sunday Bloody Sunday" filmed live at Red Rocks when I was just a kid. That song, and the music video that accompanied it, became one of my favorites during my teenage years. I always wanted to see a live show at Red Rocks. I have very few regrets when it comes to music but one of them is passing up two opportunities to see the Grateful Dead while Jerry Garcia was still alive. In this regard, I made a promise to myself that I would find a reason to see a show at Red Rocks in this life.

I finally broke out of my midlife slump when yoga and meditation became an everyday part of my life. These activities gave me comfort, tranquility and perspective. Thereafter, I noticed a further improvement in my outlook and well-being when I became a vegetarian. Then, another life improvement occurred after I became mostly vegan. Changing my daily routine, lifestyle and diet were important, but so was changing the music I listened to.

I replaced Mumford & Sons with Bruce Springsteen and the E Street Band in my music rotation. It had been years since I had listened to Springsteen on a regular basis and it felt so good to hear his voice and his music once again. At this point in time, Springsteen was releasing live soundboard recordings of most of his concerts and I listened to countless live Bruce shows during this transformative period in my life.

I was only four years old in 1978 when Springsteen released *Darkness on the Edge of Town*. Surprisingly, even though I was just a little kid, that album left a big impression on me. As the years went by, I continued to listen to that album. Over time, the themes and the songs on that record began to take on more meaning to me. Underlying many of Springsteen's songs is a message of hope. When I got back into Bruce Springsteen in 2015, "The Promised Land" once again became my personal theme song. I believe doing so helped me turn my life around.

The lyrics of "The Promise Land" paint a vivid image in my mind when Springsteen sings, "On a rattlesnake speedway in the Utah desert." I can envision Bruce and his bandmates on a spiritual vision quest together. They climb and reach the mountaintop to receive sacred knowledge from the Music

JONATHAN FINK

Gods. As they descend the mountain, they find themselves lost in the dry sand of the Utah desert. I get the feeling that the group is going through its own midlife crisis in the beginning of the song, but they carry on.

Perhaps Springsteen is recalling his early days performing in front of small crowds in mostly empty venues when he first started out on his road to the show. As he searched his soul in that Utah desert, maybe he found himself and regained his life's purpose. After suffering through the hard times, he was ready to continue his quest. He would take charge and nothing would stop him from achieving his life's goals.

In the documentary *The Promise: The Making of Darkness On the Edge of Town*, Springsteen said the song "The Promised Land" reflected what was happening in his life. It was a song about the crisis he was facing in his musical career. He said that he was unable to record a new album due to a lawsuit. He said that he felt weak. And he said he felt that he was not in control of his own life and music career. "The Promise Land" reflected his sense of despair, but also his resilience, determination and desire to transcend his limitations. The song conveys a belief that you must keep going because there is something better down the road.

I knew the Music Gods were sending me a sign that my midlife crisis was over just before my 44th birthday when Springsteen surprisingly added an extra date to his 2016 *River Tour*. The date was Thursday, April 7th and the extra performance would be at the Sprint Center in Kansas City. That extra date made it possible for my son Nate to see his first Springsteen show. The show was terrific and it was especially pleasing for me as the band segued perfectly from song to

76

THE MUSIC GODS ARE REAL VOL. 1

song throughout the show, even during the encore, just like a jamband. Here is the setlist from that memorable performance.

Bruce Springsteen & the E Street Band: 4/7/16 – Sprint Center, Kansas City, MO

I: Meet me in the City, The Ties That Bind>Sherry Darling>Jackson Cage>Two Hearts, Independence Day, Hungry Heart>Out in the Street>Crush on You>You Can Look (But You Better Not Touch), I Wanna Marry You, The River, Point Blank, Cadillac Ranch>I'm a Rocker, Fade Away, Stolen Car, Ramrod>The Price You Pay, Drive All Night, Wreck on the Highway, Badlands>No Surrender>Candy's Room>Because the Night>She's the One>Backstreets> Thunder Road

E: Born to Run>Dancing in the Dark>Rosalita (Come Out Tonight)>Tenth Avenue Freeze-Out>Shout>Bobby Jean

Springsteen adding an unplanned show in Kansas City just before my birthday was a very special wink from the universe and no doubt a birthday gift from the Music Gods.

CHAPTER FIFTEEN

The Torch

"Fruit Salad, Yummy, Yummy."
— The Wiggles

WHILE I WAS GOING THROUGH MY MIDLIFE CRISIS, Twiddle was emerging from their own existential crisis. After touring relentlessly for most of a decade, the band found themselves somewhat lost, both individually and collectively. Rather than quit the music business, they decided to keep grinding away on their road to the show. As Bruce Springsteen did before he became a music icon, Twiddle decided that they needed to make a change and go in a new direction with their management.

The band found their new manager the same way that Springsteen found his manager Jon Landau. Kevin Rondeau was a fan of the band. Rondeau and his best friend, Daniel Travis, who sometime later became Twiddle's road manager, grew up together in Connecticut. They both loved music and especially enjoyed attending live shows. Rondeau saw his first Twiddle show at The Bitter End in Bridgeport. Shortly

THE MUSIC GODS ARE REAL VOL. 1

thereafter, Rondeau and Travis started attending as many Twiddle shows as they could in New York, New Jersey and Connecticut. Back in those early days, Twiddle would play small clubs and bars in the tri-state area and, taking a page out of the Phish playbook, would hang out with their fans before and after shows. As Rondeau and Travis travelled from show to show to see Twiddle perform, their relationship with the members of the band grew. Over time, they evolved from being loyal fans, to becoming friends, and a few years later, when Twiddle parted ways with their manager, the band asked Rondeau if he wanted the job. It didn't take very long for him to accept this new position.

When Kevin Rondeau agreed to become Twiddle's manager, the band was not making any money and they could not pay him a salary. He was employed as a high school Social Studies teacher at that time, a good job with a regular paycheck. Rondeau kept his day job and for the next five years, he worked for Twiddle for free. He worked hard before and after class to book gigs for the band, and would also try to find time during the school day to do so as well. In class, Rondeau would find every opportunity to get on his laptop and book shows while his students were working independently on projects or watching a documentary or educational film.

Since the band was not on the radar of major record labels, Kevin Rondeau found a creative way to raise money for the band so they could record and produce their albums. Rondeau set up a Twiddle Kickstarter page and asked the band's fans to help raise money to pay for recording sessions. That's how the band produced *Somewhere on the Mountain*. Seventy-three backers pledged $5,596 to bring that album project to life. The band used Kickstarter again a few years later when they needed funding to record their double album *Plump*. For this double album, Twiddle raised the needed funds in just 24 hours.

As the band began to tour outside of the local region, Kevin Rondeau asked Dan Travis to join the team as the band's road manager so he could spend more time and focus on band management and booking shows. Things began improving for Twiddle in 2012 when Rondeau got the band their big break by booking them a gig at the *Gathering of the Vibes Festival* held every summer in Connecticut. Shortly thereafter in 2013, Travis went on the road with Twiddle full time.

As the good vibes began to flow back into Mihali's and Ryan Dempsey's lives, their songwriting began to flourish like never before. Dempsey channeled his inner Beethoven and wrote some unique and compelling instrumental compositions that were ideal for jamming. Meanwhile, Mihali learned to channel his personal suffering into his melodic and emotional songwriting with new songs such as "Lost in the Cold," "When it Rains it Pours" and "Amydst the Myst." After finding happiness again in his life, Mihali wrote some catchy, melodic songs about positivity, spirituality, mindfulness and persevering through life's struggles, such as "White Light," "Syncopated Healing," "Bronze Fingers," "Burdens Blooming" and "River Drift."

Now, with a great management team, a deep portfolio of songs, and a renewed passion for life, Twiddle reggae-jammed their way across the country and began turning heads like never before. Each time Twiddle returned to play a city on the East Coast, they were getting booked at bigger venues. By the summer of 2015, Twiddle was thriving as a band and finally picking up speed on their road to the show. Twiddle was now making enough money to expand their crew, so they hired Kyle Travis, Dan's cousin, to become Mihali's full-time guitar tech.

At the same time, I too was picking up speed on my own road to the show. The Kansas City Royals had just won the World Series, I had started my own investment firm, and my yoga and meditation practice kept the good vibrations flowing my way. By the beginning of summer of 2016, the Music Gods felt that I was ready for a new soundtrack to my life. In July of that year, Twiddle hosted their first music festival in Vermont and named it *Tumble Down*. The two days of music included many of Twiddle's favorite bands and Twiddle played multiple sets throughout the festival. After a long weekend of music, Twiddle emerged on stage for their last set, which was the final set of the festival.

That final set began with "Hattie's Jam" which was introduced by guest keyboard player Holly Bowling, who was sitting in with the band for the finale. Slowly, Bowling blended in with the full band as they gently segued into "When it Rains it Pours." When the band played this song, they broke it down after the second chorus, as they often do, and very slowly built up into a passionate jam before returning to the triumphant final chorus. Fellow keyboard player Dempsey usually leads this jam, but on this special occasion surprise guest Page McConnell, the keyboard player from Phish, came out on stage to lead the jam with the band.

The look on Ryan Dempsey's face was priceless. There he was, standing on stage right next to one of his music heroes. It was a mixture of awe, disbelief and humble pride. After Page

JONATHAN FINK

McConnell absolutely nailed the solo on piano, Dempsey joined Page on the organ as the band played on and finished the jam. After watching the video of Page's sit-in with Twiddle at *Tumble Down* on YouTube, I went on my nugs.net app and found another Twiddle show to listen to. While I don't remember the specific show, I do remember the first song of the first set was "Earth Mama." The song included a truly breathtaking jam and I recall thinking that Twiddle would become the next great jamband. The lyrics of "Earth Mama" also really got my attention, especially the catchy, heartwarming chorus:

> And that's the way it goes. Yeah the seasons keep on turning while our loved ones seem to grow. It's just time my friend we all gots in the end. So laugh out loud, go hug your mom. Give your girl a little kiss while you sing her this song. Go and pet your dog. Give your dad a high five. Call your brother or your sister let them know that you're alive. Then raise your glasses to the sky. Yeah this is my toast to livin' up a good life.

While I have been a passionate Twiddle fan since the *Tumble Down Festival* in July 2016, I would not see my first Twiddle show in person until February 2019. I have seen the band perform several times since, and their shows are fabulous. I'll never forget my first Twiddle show and I'm sure my wonderful daughter Kayla will never forget her first live show — the Wiggles.

The Wiggles are an Australian children's music group formed in 1991 in Sydney, Australia. They had a hit television show and Kayla was obsessed with this band. The original

THE MUSIC GODS ARE REAL VOL. 1

members of the Wiggles began their road to the show playing in traditional rock and roll bands in the 1980s. One of their former bands was called the Cockroaches. Needless to say, that band did not achieve any commercial success. Perhaps it was a poor choice of a band name. They probably would have had better luck just randomly picking their name out of the dictionary as did the Grateful Dead and Twiddle.

After years of struggling to make it in the very competitive music business, Anthony Field, the Wiggles' lead singer, was ready to quit music and get a regular nine-to-five job. He thought about becoming a preschool teacher. Before he gave up playing the guitar, Field was inspired by watching children dancing and wrote a song called "Get Ready to Wiggle." That's when he got the brilliant idea to write and record children's music that was based on educational themes.

The Wiggles began touring to promote their first children's album. The band became so successful that all of the members of the group quit their part-time day jobs to perform full time. The group augmented their act with characters, such as Dorothy the Dinosaur, Henry the Octopus, Wags the Dog and Captain Feathersword, designed, of course, to appeal to young kids. All these Wiggles characters each had their own songs. When the Wiggles TV show made it onto the airways in the United States, the band's popularity skyrocketed. The Wiggles have gone on to sell more than 23 million DVDs and 7 million albums. The Wiggles definitely made it on their road to the show.

For Kayla's first concert, to see the Wiggles perform in person, we drove from our home in Somers, New York, in Westchester County, to Bridgeport, Connecticut. Yes, we travelled a long distance to the show, just like a Deadhead or a Phishhead. The Wiggles did not disappoint. The band danced and sang all of Kayla's favorite songs, such as "Big Red Car," "Hot Potato," "I'm Dorothy the Dinosaur" and their most popular song, "Fruit Salad." Perhaps listening to "Fruit Salad" over and over again is the reason Kayla is now a vegan. The song starts with its very simple catchy chorus, "Fruit Salad, Yummy, Yummy." Then the first verse tells you how much fun it is to eat fruit. "Let's make some fruit salad today (Uh huh uh). It's fun to do it the healthy way (Uh huh uh). Take all the fruit that you want to eat. It's gonna be a fruit salad treat!" Eventually, Kayla got older and moved on from the Wiggles when she discovered the hit TV show *Hannah Montana*.

The show *Hannah Montana* follows a character named Miley Stewart, portrayed by the very talented actress/singer Miley Cyrus, who is a teenager living a double life as an average schoolgirl by day and as the famous recording artist *Hannah Montana* by night. Only a few people know of Hannah's secret alter ego. The show was such a success that Cyrus toured the country as "*Hannah Montana*." When the tour came to the New York area, Kayla had to go see her favorite TV character. *Hannah Montana* played all of Kayla's favorite songs like "The Best of Both Worlds," "Nobody's Perfect" and "Pumpin' up the Party." *Hannah Montana* was a big part of Kayla's life during her run. After Hanna Montana, Kayla moved on to the extremely popular and talented singer/songwriter Taylor Swift.

For Kayla's birthday gift, we surprised her with tickets to see Swift perform at the Prudential Center in Newark, New

THE MUSIC GODS ARE REAL VOL. 1

Jersey. Yes, another long road trip to see a show. Kayla's Taylor Swift phase lasted for a few years and we even got to see Swift perform another show, this time at the Sprint Center in Kansas City after we relocated in 2012.

Kayla's taste in music changed after she dipped into her birthday money savings to purchase a monthly subscription to Spotify Premium. Kayla now had the entire universe of music at her fingertips. Despite being raised on the Wiggles, followed by her pop music *Hannah Montana* and Taylor Swift phases, as a teenager she fell in love with rap music. My son, Nate, also had a musical upbringing but he did not follow the same path as Kayla. While Kayla preferred the Wiggles as a kid, Nate preferred to listen to Phish.

I might have played a role in this because I often played Phish in the car transporting Nate from place to place. Until he was ten years old, Nate went to sleep every night listening to the beautiful Phish song "Divided Sky." As Nate got a little older, he went to bed listening to full soundboard recordings of Phish shows. As soon as I could get away with it, I started bringing Nate with me to Phish concerts. The first Phish show Nate attended was *Festival 8*, held at the Polo Grounds in Indio, California, where the *Coachella Music* and *Stagecoach Festival* is hosted. I brought Nate to hear Phish's afternoon acoustic set.

Phish: 10/31/09 – Empire Polo Club, Indio, CA

I: Water in the Sky, Back on the Train, Brian and Robert, Invisible, Strange Design, Mountains in the Mist, The Curtain With, Army of One, Sleep Again, My Sweet One, Let Me Lie,

JONATHAN FINK

Bouncing Around the Room, Train Song, Wilson> McGrupp
and the Watchful Hosemasters

E: Driver, Talk, Secret Smile

The next Phish show Nate got to see was two years later
at *Super Ball IX*, another three-day Phish festival which took
place in Watkins Glen, New York, beginning on July 1, 2011.
Nate and I drove up from our home in Armonk for the last
day of the festival. Since the concert was so far away from
home, we spent the night in a hotel. I'll never forget that show.
We had a great day hanging out with my friends and we even
got to spent time with Reggie's cousin Ira Lindenberg, another
die-hard Phish fan who made the trip down from Toronto,
Canada. Phish played in front of an estimated 30,000 fans
and Nate and I got lost in the music and the crowd. It was
the first concert to take place at Watkins Glen International
Grand Prix Raceway since July 28, 1973. On that day almost
a half century ago, an estimated 600,000 rock fans came to
see the Allman Brothers Band, the Grateful Dead and the
Band perform. Bringing music back to this site must have
pleased the Music Gods.

The Music Gods were probably also pleased with me
because of my bold move to take Nate on his first music road
trip. Nate was just five-year-old at the time. These days, Nate
and I mostly travel to minor league baseball stadiums on our
"Baseball Gods" adventures, often following my friend and
colleague Jon Perrin. But we actually got our start traveling
together with overnight stays to see Phish in concert.

86

THE MUSIC GODS ARE REAL VOL. 1

Halfway through the second set during the song "Ghost," I convinced Nate that we needed to leave because it was getting late. We agreed to leave after the song was over. While we were waiting for that song to end, the band segued and jammed into one of Nate's favorite Phish songs, "Gotta Jibboo." As Nate heard the jam move into the familiar melody of the song, he yelled out with excitement, "Dad! Gotta Jibboo, Gotta Jibboo!" We were already slowly working our way toward the exit when Nate grabbed my hand and literally dragged me back into the crowd to fully enjoy the song. After Phish played "Gotta Jibboo," they jammed into "Light." After "Light," the band took a brief break between songs and we finally made our way towards the exit into the parking lot. Nate and I will remember that day forever, and the setlist as well.

Phish: 7/3/11 – *Super Ball IX* Festival, Watkins Glen, NY

I: Soul Shakedown Party > AC/DC Bag > The Curtain > Colonel Forbin's Ascent > Fly Famous Mockingbird > Destiny Unbound > Big Black Furry Creature from Mars, Wilson > Mound, A Song I Heard the Ocean Sing, Time Loves a Hero, Reba-> David Bowie

II: Big Balls > Down with Disease -> No Quarter > Party Time, Ghost > Gotta Jibboo > Light, Waves > What's the Use? > Meatstick > Stealing Time From the Faulty Plan, The Star Spangled Banner

E: First Tube

JONATHAN FINK

As was the case with Kayla, Nate's musical tastes began to drift as he got older. Despite being raised on Phish, his favorite band as a kid was a fictitious boy band called "Big Time Rush" from a popular television show. Sound familiar? Recall that Kayla first fell in love with the Wiggles on TV and then progressed to the fictitious TV show singer "*Hannah Montana.*" Well done Nickelodeon, well done. Big Time Rush also played the Sprint Center after we moved to Kansas City in 2012. Of course, we took Nate to see them as a gift for his birthday.

A few years later, Nate really got into pop music. When Ross Lynch, the star of the kids' TV show *Austin & Ally*, started his own band with his siblings called "R5," Nate became obsessed with that band. Nate got to see R5 in person months later when their tour came to Kansas City. After the boy band and pop music phases, Nate discovered what Kayla had known for some time, rap music was where it's at. Now I had two kids obsessed with hip hop!

For me it was all coming full circle. I recall in middle school discovering rap music. All my friends and I wanted to be rappers and learn how to break dance. First, I listened to the Fat Boys, Whodini and Kurtis Blow. Then Run-DMC. But when my middle school friends and I discovered the Beastie Boys, we all lost our minds. We all wanted to be the Beastie Boys.

As a music lover, I am elated that Kayla and Nate share my passion for music. I am also truly pleased that they both particularly enjoy live concerts, just like me. In 2018 Kayla, Nate and I attended our first rap show together, travelling to a minor league hockey arena in Independence, Missouri, to see — Russ.

88

THE MUSIC GODS ARE REAL VOL. 1

The rapper Russ was of particular interest to me because Kayla told me that he was into the law of attraction, positivity and manifesting. After years of releasing mixtapes, Russ started putting out his music on SoundCloud recorded in his home studio using his laptop. He wrote his own lyrics, made his own beats, and mixed and mastered his own songs. He recorded eleven albums before he made it onto the radar screen of major record labels. He struggled to get air play for the first ten years of his career, but he never gave up on his dreams. As Russ started learning and using the law of attraction, his music career took off. Russ' mindset of positive thinking and manifesting his thoughts into reality is truly inspiring.

Russ put on a great show the night we saw him perform. During the show, he gave a few inspirational speeches about following your dreams and not letting the negativity of people around you, including even your own parents, get in the way of your dreams. He encouraged his fans to find out what they were passionate about and then instructed them to pursue that dream with all of their hearts. His main theme during the show was believing in yourself and ignoring the disbelievers and haters. I have followed Russ on his road to the show. He played a sold-out Staples Center in Los Angeles in 2018, selling out all 21,000 seats. He recently performed in Brazil and also played a show in Egypt. Russ has gone global and is clearly on his way to stardom. Russ, may the Music Gods always be with you! As we walked out of that concert, I knew that I had successfully passed the torch and my love of live music on to my children.

CHAPTER SIXTEEN

The Dolores Cannon Method

"It has been said that once the mind has been expanded by an idea
or concept, it can never return to its original way of thinking."
— Dolores Cannon

PAST LIFE REGRESSIONIST DOLORES CANNON PASSED
away in 2014 but her legacy lives on in her books and with the
legion of students who now practice her hypnotherapy method
worldwide. She spent the better part of her life traveling the
world doing sessions for clients and teaching her method to
students during her workshops. Cannon's technique for past
life regression is known as "Quantum Healing Hypnosis."

When I first discovered the Dolores Cannon Method on
YouTube, I was fascinated and wanted to learn as much about
it as I could. With the help of the internet, I located many of
Cannon's speeches and interviews with past life regressionists
who embraced her method. Then, when I found out that my
friend and fellow author Cathy Byrd's past life regressionist
Jeroen de Wit was a former student of Dolores Cannon and
also used the Quantum Healing Hypnosis method, I knew that

THE MUSIC GODS ARE REAL VOL. 1

it was only a matter of time before the Music Gods would arrange for me to meet him.

I went through a phase during which I searched using my podcast app for a specific word that I wanted to explore and learn more about. Sometimes I typed in the phrase past life regression, sometimes astrology, and one time I typed in "Kundalini," a Sanskrit word used in yoga. I discovered an interview with a Kundalini yoga instructor on a podcast called *The Balanced Blonde*. The interview was interesting and enjoyable so I subscribed to the podcast to catch future episodes.

One day our family was driving in the car to my grandparents' house when Kayla mentioned that she had just listened to Cathy Byrd's past life regressionist being interviewed on a podcast. She told me that they talked about Cathy's book, *The Boy Who Knew Too Much*. That's when Kayla and I realized that we both had been listening to the same podcast at the same time. Much to my surprise, Kayla had discovered *The Balanced Blonde* on Instagram at about the same time I did and she also downloaded the podcast. That night I listened to The Balanced Blonde's interview with Jeroen de Wit. The Music Gods were preparing me to meet this past life regressionist.

I am usually the spontaneous one in my family. However, the Music Gods must have influenced my wife, Reggie, because one day at dinner she randomly suggested that we plan a quick vacation to Los Angeles before school started. We all thought it was a great idea, so Reggie booked the trip and a few days later off we flew to LAX airport. The first night at dinner in Los Angeles, we mapped out our plans for the week. Each family member took a turn to say what he or she wanted to

91

do while in LA. After all of the plans were put on our agenda, there was one afternoon remaining without a designated activity. I asked Reggie and the kids if they would mind if I tried to book a session with Jeroen de Wit since we happened to be in town. They said sure.

I contacted Jeroen to see if he could find time to meet with me on such short notice. The Music Gods must have intervened because an appointment had just canceled and he was able to fit me into his schedule. I arrived early for my appointment at Jeroen's home and went around to the backyard where he had a small hut where he does his sessions. Just outside of the hut I saw a small fountain sprinkling water, delivering a very soothing vibration and delightful sound. After a few minutes, Jeroen came out to greet me.

Jeroen spent ample time interviewing me before the session. Then I laid down on what looked like a massage table and Jeroen wrapped me in clean white sheets and tucked me tight into a blanket. The session was recorded on video and I received a copy the next day via an email link.

I must admit it was weird seeing myself on video in that hypnotic trance. Every time Jeroen would ask me a question, I could see my eyes moving behind my closed eyelids as I was searching for answers. Just like the disclaimer in my first book, *The Baseball Gods are Real*, when I described what I saw during a wonderful floating meditation session, the images in my mind that I saw during hypnosis could simply be my wild imagination at work. Perhaps it was my subconscious mind. And maybe, just maybe, I was getting a glimpse of a past life.

I was deep in a meditative, hypnotic state when Jeroen asked me to imagine rising into the clouds and traveling

THE MUSIC GODS ARE REAL VOL. 1

through time and space to get a glimpse of a past life. When my soul or higher self was ready to proceed, I descended from the clouds and saw myself as a young Native American boy. At the time, I could not tell the exact location of where I was, yet I had this knowing feeling that I was in Montana. I also had this knowing feeling that I was raised by the elders in the tribe. Then, when Jeroen asked me if I could see my own death in that past life, I said I could and went on to describe my death. I was a young boy, perhaps a teenager, inflicted with some kind of terribly contagious disease for which there was no cure. The tribal elders decided that they had to get rid of me for fear that I would get other members of the tribe sick. The only solution was to kill me.

Following the orders of the elders, the tribe members prepared a ceremony for me and built a bed of fire made out of wood, sticks and tree branches. When the ceremony started, tribesmen carried me and placed my body on the bed of fire. The tribe members sang, chanted, beat their drums and danced in circles all around me. Then, the tribe's medicine man set my makeshift bed of wood, branches and leaves ablaze.

During this past life regression session, I was even able to recall the thoughts that the little Native American boy had as he began to pass from life on earth to the spirit world. It was time to leave this sick body of mine. I did not want to get anyone else sick and was willing to be sacrificed for the good of the tribe. I felt no pain as I left my body and ascended towards the beautiful, blissful white light above. Ever since this truly extraordinary session with Jeroen de Wit, I have been thinking about — Montana.

93

CHAPTER SEVENTEEN

The Road to Montana

"There's so much more to every soul."
— Twiddle

SOON AFTER MY REMARKABLE PAST LIFE REGRESSION session experience with Jeroen de Wit, I asked Reggie if she would be willing to go on a family summer vacation to Montana. She was not thrilled with the idea. A few days later, I casually asked Reggie during dinner what she thought about going on a ski vacation to Montana next winter. She politely replied that going on a ski vacation to Montana would not be her first choice. Then a few weeks after that, while we were planning a vacation to celebrate our twentieth wedding anniversary, I humorously suggested that we go to a quiet, romantic hideaway in the hills of Montana. She just rolled her eyes. I jokingly said, "Ok, well one of these days I am going to Montana, even if I have to go alone. I may just pray to the Music Gods."

The next day I attended a hot yoga class and after meditation at the end of the session, I prayed. In my mind I said these

94

words, "Spirit Guides, Guardian Angels, Ascended Masters, Higher Self, I thank you, I thank you, I thank you, I thank you. Please protect me with everything I say, everything I do, and everywhere I go." Then I prayed, "And please give me an excuse to go to Montana so I can validate my past life as a Native American boy." I went to a second hot yoga class that evening, this time with Kayla, and prayed about going to Montana again.

The next day I did a long meditation session first thing in the morning. For thirty minutes straight, I repeated over and over and over in my mind the Sanskrit phrase "sat nam." In Sanskrit, sat nam means "There is one God." The word "sat" means "true/everlasting," and "nam" means "name." Another interpretation of this phrase is "whose name is truth." Sat nam can also be interpreted to mean "I am truth." Since I had no business meetings scheduled for that day and the stock market was tame, I attended another hot yoga class during the lunch hour at Core Power Yoga, located just down the street from my home. I ordered a veggie burger at Houlihan's after yoga class and as I waited for my food to arrive, I got the idea to write a series of books entitled *The Music Gods are Real*.

It continues to amaze me how these ideas seem to flow to me in such abundance during periods when I am most dedicated to my practice of yoga and meditation. That night during another meditation session, it occurred to me that I should interview a band for my first music book. I had interviewed veteran pitcher Tim Dillard for my second book about baseball, *The Baseball Gods are Real - Volume 2: The Road to the Show*, and I had recently interviewed the greatest ballhawk of all time, Zack Hample, for my yet unpublished third

JONATHAN FINK

Baseball Gods book, *The Baseball Gods are Real - Volume 3: The Religion of Baseball*. I felt that both interviews added a nice dimension to each book. As I thought about which band would be great to interview, I immediately realized that it had to be Twiddle, my new favorite band.

Perhaps it was a coincidence, but the very next day Twiddle announced its *2019 Winter Tour*. Not only was the band scheduled to play a date in Kansas City, Twiddle's tour would traverse along the West Coast and conclude with a run through the Pacific Northwest and northern Rocky Mountains, including two shows in, you guessed it, Montana. I could not believe my eyes. The Music Gods must have been very pleased with themselves.

Now here is where the story gets downright spooky or miraculous, depending on your perspective. It was a synchronicity I simply could not ignore. The day after the Twiddle *2019 Winter Tour* was announced, I went to the dentist and brought signed copies of my first Baseball Gods book to give to the receptionist, the dentist and the dental hygienist. When Lauren, the dental hygienist, received her signed copy, she quickly read the back cover, excitedly said she couldn't wait to read it, and told me that she and her husband were seriously interested in spirituality. I casually asked her how that happened and she began to tell me a story that sounded fascinating. Unfortunately, she had another dental patient to attend to and couldn't finish telling me the tale. Subsequently, I learned that Lauren's husband, Mike, had come home from work early that afternoon and had seen my Baseball Gods book on the kitchen table. He read it cover to cover that night. The next day he called me and suggested that we meet for lunch.

THE MUSIC GODS ARE REAL VOL. 1

At lunch the following day, Mike and I shared our life stories and our views on spirituality. I asked Mike to tell me more about the story his wife, Lauren, had started telling me in the dental office. Mike told me that during his sophomore year at college in California, he'd read a book entitled *Yellowtail: Crow Medicine Man and Sun Dance Chief: An Autobiography*. Mike was so moved by the book that he got in his car and drove straight to the Indian reservation just outside of Billings, Montana, looking to meet the medicine man himself, Yellowtail. To Mike's disappointment and sadness, Yellowtail had recently passed away. Mike was taken to meet Yellowtail's successor instead.

Mike was offered dinner and a place to sleep on the reservation for the night. Days turned into weeks. Weeks turned into months. Months turned into years. Mike lived in Montana with the Crow tribe for the next four years. He was adopted by a Crow family and given a Crow name. He worked odd jobs and helped the tribe in any way that he could. Mike learned the ways of the Crow, including building sweat lodges and participating in the annual Crow Sundance festival, where he danced for three days straight without food. Mike said that the time he spent in Montana as a member of the Crow nation was a truly amazing, life changing experience.

Mike also told me that he even went on a vision quest, a rite of passage for a teenage Native American boy. Mike said that when a member of the tribe turns thirteen, he is sent off into the wilderness for three days without food. Fasting was part of the vision quest. After three days out on his own in the wilderness, the boy returns home to his tribe, assuming he survives the fast, the wilderness, the bears and the wolves, ready to

97

assume adult responsibilities. Obviously, Mike survived his vision quest.

I was fascinated to learn from Mike that the most sacred number to the Crow tribe is the number four. Four has been my favorite number since I was a little kid. Perhaps that's why I have always mysteriously loved that number. The other sacred number to the Crow tribe is seven.

At lunch that day Mike blew me away with his stories and life experiences. Not only did he live as a member of the Crow tribe for four years, he also served in the Marines for four years after he left Montana and the tribe. He actually signed up voluntarily shortly before the 9/11 terrorist attack on the Twin Towers in New York City. Then he was sent to Iraq. Mike also spent a few years fighting forest fires in the Pacific Northwest after he was discharged from the military. I told Mike that I hoped one day my publishing company, Polo Grounds Publishing, would get the chance to publish his life memoirs.

Changing the conversation at lunch, I told Mike that years ago I toured Europe with the rock band the Black Crowes and I managed the jamband Scarecrow Collection after college when I worked for Gelernt Music Management. I also told Mike about my past life regression session where I was a Native American boy living in Montana. Mike did not seem a bit surprised. I had a feeling that he knew that his medicine fathers had arranged our meeting.

Before we departed the restaurant, Mike suggested I read two books about the Crow tribe. The first was the book about Yellowtail previously mentioned and the second was *Plenty-Coups: Chief of the Crows*. Reading those books, I learned how I may have died in my past life as young member of the Crow tribe in Montana. In the early 1800s, a small pox epidemic almost wiped out the Crow Nation. Countless lives were lost, including many children. Probably me.

My lunch with Mike was enlightening, to say the least. As I thought about it afterwards, I had no doubt that the Music Gods would make sure that I had the opportunity to visit the Crow tribe reservation in Montana.

CHAPTER EIGHTEEN

The Winter Tour

"Take all my pain and turn it into white light."
— Twiddle

IN AN ATTEMPT TO JUSTIFY MY TRIP TO MONTANA, I decided first to put the Music Gods to the test. The Baseball Gods had earned my trust over the last few years and now I needed to find out if the Music Gods were also real. I told Reggie that I would make every effort to arrange an interview with Twiddle and, as crazy as it sounds, meet and interview the band in Montana. I told Reggie that if I was unsuccessful in getting the interviews scheduled before Twiddle's *2019 Winter Tour* reached Kansas City, I would forego my vision quest to the Crow tribe reservation outside of Billings, Montana. I felt that if I didn't connect with Twiddle before they arrived in Kansas City, then perhaps my idea to interview the band was just not meant to be.

I did some research and located Twiddle's manager, Kevin Rondeau, on LinkedIn, the business-related social network. I

100

THE MUSIC GODS ARE REAL VOL. 1

sent him an email to introduce myself and explain why I wanted to get in touch with him. I did not hear back from him after a few days, so I tried again also without success. Continuing my pursuit, I also located Rondeau on Facebook and sent him a message. I pasted a link to an article about my baseball book to show him that I was a serious, successful author.

Kevin Rondeau responded to my Facebook post and suggested that I send a formal email to the band's official manager email address, so I did. That afternoon during meditation session, the thought came to me that I should mail a signed copy of my book to Rondeau and send signed copies to everyone in the band and crew as well. So off to the post office I went, to mail a total of twelve signed books to Rondeau at Twiddle's business office.

A week later I received an email from Kevin Rondeau informing me that the band was excited to be interviewed for my Music Gods book. I had successfully manifested this reality. The best part of the email was that Rondeau said that the interviews could be scheduled during the time the band would be in Montana. And there it was. My confirmation, without a shadow of a doubt — The Music Gods Are Real.

Shortly thereafter, I received an email from Dan Travis, Twiddle's tour and business manager. Travis offered to add me to the guest list for the band's Kansas City show. He also permitted me to invite Jon Perrin and his girlfriend and my good friend Paul Greenwood to join me at the performance. Travis also mentioned in his email that while we would do interviews in Montana, if there was the time, he would also try to arrange some interviews while the band was in Kansas City.

Avid Twiddle fans could tell right away from the setlists

101

that the band's 2019 *Winter Tour* was different from the music they last played on New Year's Eve in Boston. It seemed as if they had received a cosmic download from the universe. The band was playing with newfound chemistry and jamming in and out of songs with amazing precision. They sounded better than ever. The band could always jam, but now they were doing so with incredible setlist creativity. It was as if Twiddle was channeling Phish from 1994, but doing it their way.

Each night of the tour had groundbreaking creativity. Not only were Twiddle's setlists especially imaginative and extremely well played, the band had so much great material that they did not repeat any songs during the first four performances on the tour. To help the band keep their streak going, I posted on Twitter a suggested setlist for the band to consider with songs they had not yet played on the tour. Believe it or not, the streak continued in Kansas City. This was amazing.

The following night in Iowa City, after 11 consecutive sets and 73 songs without a repeat, the "Twiddle no-repeat" streak came to an end. This tour for Twiddle was clearly different from all of their previous tours. The band was now peaking, jamming their very best. You could feel the difference right from the first note of the first set of tour. And the band seemed to have a newfound appreciation for setlist design.

The fact that Twiddle was playing so well was remarkable because two nights before the tour started, Ryan Dempsey broke two bones in his right leg. The doctor recommended surgery, but with the tour scheduled to start in just two days, Dempsey decided to wear a boot, endure the pain, and as they say in baseball, "take one for the team." Dempsey began the tour in a wheelchair in considerable pain but emotionally rallied each night of the tour just before showtime, slipping

THE MUSIC GODS ARE REAL VOL. 1

off his walking boot and playing the show as best he could. Not only did Dempsey play extraordinarily well, but Twiddle sounded even better than ever before.

The first night of the Twiddle 2019 *Winter Tour* began on January 30, 2019, at George's Majestic Lounge in Fayetteville, Arkansas. To make sure the tour's opening performance was extraordinary, the band filled the show with covers and original songs related to the state of Arkansas. Twiddle played "Apples" because the apple blossom is the state flower of Arkansas. They covered John Denver's "Country Roads." They played "Milk" because milk is the official beverage of Arkansas. Cleverly, they played "The Fantastic Tale of Ricky Snickle" because the main character in the song was born in Little Rock, the state capital of Arkansas. Twiddle played "Gatsby the Great" because Arkansas is home to the World Championship Duck Calling Contest. Twiddle even played "Honeyburste" and "Beehop" because the honey bee is the official state insect of Arkansas. Here is the setlist from Twiddle's memorable performance in Fayetteville.

Twiddle: 1/30/19 - George's Majestic Lounge, Fayetteville, AR

I: Apples> Funkytown> Apples> River Drift, Invisible Ink> Take Me Home, Country Roads> Invisible Ink, Milk, The Fantastic Tale Of Ricky Snickle

II: Gatsby The Great> Polluted Beauty> Gatsby The Great, Honeyburste> Beehop, Ganja Medley, Second Wind> Eyes Of The World

E: Mad World

JONATHAN FINK

I'm sure both the screaming Twiddle fans in Fayetteville and the Music Gods were pleased with the way Twiddle began their tour.

Before making their way to Kansas City, Twiddle played a three-night run across Texas in Dallas, Houston and Austin. The setlist creativity continued at each venue, including a debut mashup of original songs, "Jamflowman" and "Carter Candlestick." The band busted out a "Lord of the Rings" themed jam one night and a "Harry Potter" themed jam another night. They also mashed together the songs "Subconscious Prelude" and "Indigo Trigger." They even played the song "Syncopated Healing," backwards!

When photographer and music beat writer Brittany NO FOMO caught up with the band during their swing through Texas, she asked Mihali about the creative setlists and song arrangements on this tour for inclusion in her 2019 *Live for Live Music* article, "What Twiddle Tour Means for The Jam Scene in Texas." Savoulidis noted, "We've definitely tried out a few new things on this tour, and it's been awesome that it was received so well in Texas. The energy and response from all of those cities was amazing." Here are the setlists for Twiddle's shows in Dallas, Houston and Austin.

Twiddle: 1/31/19 - Deep Ellum Art Co., Dallas, TX

I: Nicodemus Portulay, Subconscious Prelude > Indigo Trigger, Peas And Carrots, Mamunes The Faun, Blunderbuss

II: White Light, New Sun> Syncopated Healing, Moments, Atlantic Mocean>Barbeque> Atlantic Mocean

E: Folsom Prison Blues

THE MUSIC GODS ARE REAL VOL. 1

Twiddle: 2/1/19 - Last Concert Cafe, Houston, TX

I: Every Soul> Best Feeling> Every Soul, The Caterpillar, Fat Country Baby>Hattibagen McRat> Cabbage Face

II: Machine, Tiberius> Classical Gas> Tiberius, Latin Tang, Beethoven and Greene>Frankenfoote

E: Lost in The Cold

Twiddle: 2/2/19 – Antone's, Austin, TX

I: Orlando's> Rocky Raccoon> Orlando's> Jamflowman> Carter Candlestick> Zazu's Flight> Jamflowman

II: Dr. Remidi's Melodium, Amydst The Myst, Daydream Farmer, D'yer Mak'er, Wasabi Eruption> The Box

E: Hatti's Jam> When It Rains It Pours

The next stop for Twiddle was Kansas City. Even though the band had played before at many legendary venues, I would suggest that performing in my home town may have been the most significant performance of all. That's where the band played a small but very well-known venue that has its own music prophecy and a track record to prove it. Twiddle performed at — the recordBar.

CHAPTER NINETEEN

The recordBar Prophecy

"So many good things come to those who love relentlessly."
— Twiddle

TWIDDLE WAS RIDING HIGH AFTER PLAYING ANOTHER
sold-out show in Austin, TX. The next day the band and
their crew rolled into Kansas City to play a rarely scheduled Monday night show. It was also the night after the New
England Patriots won another Super Bowl with the great Tom
Brady at the helm. Despite the band's success so far on the
tour, I thought that this show would be a good litmus test.

Doing yoga at the 9 a.m. class that day, I got the idea to
send Kevin Rondeau and Dan Travis an email welcoming
them to Kansas City. In the email, I suggested a couple of
great barbeque restaurants near the venue, Arthur Bryant's
and Jack Stack. Having eaten in each place many times before
going vegetarian and then vegan, I know firsthand why Kansas
City is so well known for BBQ.

I arrived at the recordBar early and saw Kevin Rondeau
at the Twiddle merchandise table. I introduced myself and

106

THE MUSIC GODS ARE REAL VOL. 1

thanked him for the invitation to the show and for allowing me to interview the band. From the first minute we met, I knew that we would have a lot in common and much to discuss. During our chat, I mentioned how impressed I was with the setlists on the tour. Rondeau smiled in acknowledgement and told me that Mihali was digging deep through his song catalogue to try and keep the no-repeat streak going. I brought up my tweet suggesting songs for the band to play in Kansas City to keep their no-repeat streak alive. Rondeau said that he and the band had seen that tweet and they liked my suggestions.

As Kevin Rondeau and I were talking about the band's no-repeat song streak, Ryan Dempsey hobbled over. After Rondeau introduced us, I reiterated to Dempsey how impressed I was with Twiddle's song selections so far on this tour. Dempsey acknowledged that the current setlists had been challenging and joked that he wanted to blow the minds of their fans back home. After chatting about the difficulties of touring with a broken leg, I mentioned to Dempsey that I love reading and am often at the book store buying random books. I told him I had a book in mind that I thought would be a perfect gift for him and would give it to him when I interviewed the band in Montana. When I told Dempsey the book was about the JFK assassination and aliens, he smiled and invited me to join him outside while he smoked a cigarette.

While outside, Dempsey and I talked briefly about my Baseball Gods book. I mentioned that my book was really as much about yoga, meditation, manifesting and synchronicity as it was about baseball. Dempsey said that he lives his entire life in the moment and believing in synchronicity. He said that manifesting was a way of life for him. Then he gave me examples.

JONATHAN FINK

Ryan Dempsey had recently opened Orlando's Bar and Lounge in Burlington, Vermont. He explained how everything came together with synchronicities. The name of the bar came to him from a new Twiddle song entitled "Orlando's." He told me that he had literally manifested this new bar into existence. Then he gave me another example. He has always been a huge fan of the Grateful Dead and Phish. After years as a fan, he manifested sharing the stage with Page McConnell from Phish and did so. A few months after that, he manifested jamming on stage with Phil Lesh of the Grateful Dead and did that too. Both experiences were dreams come true for Dempsey. When it was time for Dempsey to head back inside to get ready for the concert, I wished him well and a great show and said, "See you in Montana!"

Back inside, I joked with Kevin Rondeau that I'd just had my first interview. Moments later, Mihali walked up to the merchandise table and gave us a nod, so I took the opportunity to introduce myself. I said, "Hey, nice to meet you, I'm Fink." I jokingly thanked Mihali for scheduling a tour date in Kansas City and also for the dates in Montana. I mentioned my interesting past life regression experiences, which I discussed in some detail in my first two Baseball Gods books. Then I told Mihali about my more recent past life regression session with Jeroen de Wit in Los Angeles in which I was a Native America boy living in Montana. I joked that ever since that incredible session, I had been looking for an excuse to visit Montana to try and validate this past life.

While a discussion about "past life regression" and a statement like, "I was a Native American boy in a past life" may sound very odd to the average person walking down the street,

108

THE MUSIC GODS ARE REAL VOL. 1

Mihali totally got it. In fact, he told me that his father wrote one of the first books ever about past life regression. My mind was blown and I am sure my facial expression showed how surprised and shocked I was. I was speechless. After I recovered, we gave each other a warm good-bye embrace, I wished him a great show, and then, surprisingly, he said to me, "See you in Montana."

The Twiddle concert at the recordBar that night was perfect and the band played a great setlist. They pulled it off even without playing any of their more well-known songs like "Frankenfoote," "Beethoven and Greene," "Cabbage Face," "Gatsby the Great" and "When it Rains it Pours." Here is the setlist for Twiddle's truly stellar performance at recordBar.

Twiddle: 2/4/19 – recordBar, Kansas City, MO

I: Grandpa Fox> Brick Of Barley> Grandpa Fox, Be There, Wescotton Candy, Earth Mama

II: Complacent Race, Wildfire, Burden's Blooming, Bronze Fingers> Glory, The FRENDS Theme, Brown Chicken Brown Cow

E: Tom's Song

On my way home from the concert, I thought, the next time I see Mihali, Dempsey, Gubb, Brook, Rondeau and the Travis boys will be in Missoula and Bozeman, Montana. I was already looking forward to the trip.

The next day at yoga class, the instructor, Alex Lavigne, asked me how the Twiddle show was the night before. I told her the show was perfect. Then she told me that it was good luck for bands to play at the recordBar. She said, "Yeah, so many bands have played there and like a year later, they blew up and got really big." She mentioned two music acts that had a huge jump in popularity and success after playing there. The first was Tash Sultana and the second was Coheed & Cambria. She suggested that I google it. I did and it turns out that Alex was onto something.

My research revealed that the original recordBar was located in Westport, a section of Kansas City just north of the Country Club Plaza and south of the downtown area where the Power & Light District is located. After years in Westport, the owners relocated into a bigger venue in downtown Kansas City a few blocks south of the Sprint Center. The new space had a capacity of 400, up from the recordBar's original capacity of 300.

Performing at the recordBar may indeed bring good luck. I found evidence that a few unknown bands who played there went on to achieve success very quickly thereafter. After confirming that what Alex Lavigne had told me was true, I named this phenomenon "The recordBar Prophecy." Following up further on what Alex told me, I googled Tash Sultana and found this interesting information on Wikipedia:

Tash Sultana (born 15 June 1995) is an Australian singer-songwriter and multi-instrumentalist, described as a "one-person band." Sultana's 2016 single "Jungle" was voted into third place in the Triple J Hottest 100,

THE MUSIC GODS ARE REAL VOL. 1

2016; Sultana also had three songs voted into the Triple J Hottest 100, 2017. Sultana grew up in Melbourne, and has been playing guitar from the age of three, beginning a career in music through busking. An active musician on Bandcamp since 2013, Sultana's recordings were viewed millions of times on YouTube in 2016. Sultana's EP, *Notion*, was released on 23 September 2016, followed by a sold-out world tour in early 2017.

Then I searched for Coheed & Cambria, the second act mentioned by Alex Lavigne that I had never heard of. It turns out that the band had played in Kansas City in the summer of 2018 at the Starlight Theatre, a very large outdoor venue next door to the Kansas City Zoo. I have been to Starlight three times so far, once to see Phish and twice to see Widespread Panic. Another band that played the recordBar on the verge of making it big was Phoenix. They played at the recordBar in 2009 and shortly thereafter played a free Myspace concert which was viewed by thousands of music fans. A year later Phoenix played a sold-out show at Kansas City's Uptown Theater.

Perhaps the best example of "The recordBar Prophecy" occurred on June 16, 2010. That's when a bluegrass, folk rock group from London, England, played there. You guessed it — Mumford & Sons. Without a doubt, Mumford & Sons has made it all the way on their road to the show. They have become one of the biggest bands in the world.

Twiddle's booking agent could have scheduled a show at a number of venues in the Kansas City area. There are many locations with capacity to hold 400 people, such as Knuckleheads,

111

JONATHAN FINK

The Riot Room, Crossroads, The Voodoo Lounge and The Truman. Perhaps it was just their destiny that Twiddle played the recordBar in Kansas City on their *2019 Winter Tour*. Only time will tell.

With Kansas City and their no-repeat streak behind them, Twiddle blazed through Madison, Wisconsin, Chicago, Illinois and St. Louis, Missouri, before ending the first leg of their tour with another sold-out show in Louisville, Kentucky. Then the band flew home to Vermont for a few weeks off and some rest and relaxation. After their time off in Vermont, Twiddle flew to the West Coast to begin the second leg of the tour. The band spent the entire month of March on the road travelling up the California coast with a diversion to play a festival show in Phoenix, Arizona, during the Major League Baseball spring training season. Then to end the tour, Twiddle worked their way up to the Pacific Northwest. After scheduled shows in Oregon and Washington, the band made their way to Montana.

CHAPTER TWENTY

The Vision Quest

"Take a deep breath go on a trip with me."
— Twiddle

COLLEGE KIDS LIVING IN BOULDER, COLORADO, ONE OF my favorite cities in America, seem to have it all. It's the home of the University of Colorado and the city has a loveable hippie vibe and an adorable downtown area with shops and restaurants near the campus. The city has close access to a big city like Denver yet is far enough away from that major metropolis to be surrounded by the beautiful Rocky Mountains. The mountains of Colorado are not just beautiful to look at year-round, they also provide the backdrop for great outdoor activities such as skiing in the winter and hiking in the summer. But if Boulder ever becomes overpopulated due to its awesomeness, I suggest that high school seniors applying to college consider the University of Montana in Missoula. In my opinion, charming Missoula is the next Boulder.

Flying from Kansas City to Denver and from Denver to Missoula, I was in awe of the sheer beauty and vastness of

JONATHAN FINK

the Colorado Rocky Mountain range, including the seemingly untouched wilderness of thousands and thousands of acres of pristine land covered with tall trees coated with snow. And arriving at the Missoula airport was refreshing. Rather than the hectic, crowded scene travelers often experience arriving at busy airports like LaGuardia and Kennedy in Queens, New York, Missoula International Airport is clean, quiet and peaceful, just like Kansas City's International Airport. Looking around at baggage claim waiting for my suitcase, I realized that the terminal building is basically a very large log cabin. As I traveled from the airport into Missoula, I concluded that the city is just as adorable as its log cabin airport.

I arrived early at the Top Hat music venue so I could say hello to Kevin Rondeau, who had told me to find him at the merchandise table when I arrived. After chatting about Twiddle's most recent shows on the tour, I showed Kevin Rondeau the gift I'd brought for Mihali, a Kansas City Royals baseball jersey. When I showed him the back of the jersey, Kevin smiled when he saw the number four.

It turns out that, like me, Kevin Rondeau's favorite number is four. He told me that he loves the number four so much that he even wrote a college paper about numerology, featuring the relevance of that number. He even has a tattoo on his ankle of the number four, which he showed to me. I was amazed. Another surprising synchronicity indeed.

Kevin Rondeau was equally amazed when I gave him his thank you gift for all he had done for me. It was a silver eagle coin set of — you guessed it — four coins. At the same time, I suggested that Twiddle consider merchandising silver bullion .999 coins at their shows, just like they do with posters,

T-shirts and hats. My sense was that any coins that did not sell would likely benefit the band because there would be a good chance that the value of the silver coins would increase in value over time.

I decided to grab a local Montana beer at the bar before the opening band Iya Terra, a reggae band from Los Angeles, took the stage to begin their set. As I was waiting to pay the bartender, Mihali showed up and stood right next to me at the bar. Having chatted with him just a few weeks ago in Kansas City, we picked up our conversation as if no time had passed. When I told Mihali how good I thought the winter tour sounded so far, he was appreciative and humble to receive my compliments. He replied that he was grateful that the shows sounded good to me because it isn't as easy as it looks. Behind the scenes, he said, the band had been struggling to deal with the grind of the tour.

Mihali explained that Dempsey broke his right leg just before the winter tour started. Later, on the second leg of the tour (no pun intended), he hurt his back falling down when a chair was innocently pulled away a few seconds before he sat down. Then, the flu started to spread around the Twiddle crew and the members of Iya Terra. Mihali told me that one night he was so sick with flu symptoms that he actually went to a hospital.

I redirected our conversation to a more jovial topic when I mentioned that I had brought him a Kansas City Royals baseball jersey as a gift. I told him it might be a bit cliché, but I thought it was awesome when a musician wears a sports jersey on stage. I said that the local fans love it. For example, I recalled that someone in Pigeons Playing Ping Pong recently wore a

JONATHAN FINK

Blackhawks hockey jersey while playing a show in Chicago and the crowd went wild. We joked about whether he should wear the Royals jersey in Columbia, Missouri, next month on the first night of the Road to Red Rocks tour because the city is located halfway between Kansas City and St. Louis. Mihali said that he would let me decide. I replied, "Well, if I was your manager, I'd say don't wear it in Columbia. Wait until your next Kansas City show." He joked, with a grin, that wearing it in Columbia might be a bit edgy. I agreed and we both laughed.

Changing the subject once again, I mentioned that Twiddle seemed to play two-hour shows on this tour, sometimes performing just one long set with an encore rather than two sets. Since I was used to and so much enjoyed three-hour long shows from Bruce Springsteen and jambands like Phish and Widespread Panic, we discussed the pros and cons of shorter versus longer concerts and touring solo or with an opening band. Since Mihali loves reggae music, he told me that touring with one of his favorite reggae bands, Iya Terra, was a real treat for him. He said that he wanted to make sure that Iya Terra always had a good amount of time to play their opening set, even if that meant Twiddle played a slightly shorter set due to an early venue curfew. I thought that was very considerate of Mihali.

Our conversation shifted again, this time to the themes in this Music Gods book. I said that I truly believed that Twiddle was on the verge of becoming one of the next great jambands. However, I also told him that I thought that their timeline for making it to the show may have been pushed back due to Phish reuniting and the new wave of Grateful Dead reincarnations entering the jamband music scene, flooding the market with

116

so much good music. Our chat came to an end when Iya Terra walked on stage and started to play their opening set. Mihali and I said our goodbyes and I wished him a great show.

Iya Terra's set was excellent and, seeing it in person, I knew the band was a great choice to open for Twiddle. After a short break, Twiddle came on stage and I am thrilled to report that their Missoula show was not just good, it was great. Here is the setlist for that performance.

Twiddle: 03/20/2019 – Top Hat, Missoula, MT

I: Gatsby The Great > Polluted Beauty> Subconscious Prelude> Gatsby The Great

II: Earth Mama> Round Here>Earth Mama, Tiberius>Apples>Tiberius>Funkytown>Tiberius, Daydream Farmer, Hatti's Jam> Be There

E: When It Rains It Pours

In front of a crowd of almost 400, mostly college kids, Twiddle played an outstanding show at the Top Hat. Highlights included a terrific thirty-minute version of "Gatsby The Great" to start the show. The jam included a rarely played classical music composition, "Pachelbel's Canon," which Dempsey played to perfection. After jamming out some classical music, the band easily segued into "Polluted Beauty," a song about planet earth's polluted environment. This blended perfectly into "Subconscious Prelude," a song about insomnia.

JONATHAN FINK

As the "Subconscious" jam was peaking, I thought the band was headed back into "Polluted Beauty." Instead, they jammed back into "Gatsby The Great" to finish the first set.

As good as Twiddle's first set was, their second set may have been even better. Perhaps I am somewhat biased because not only did the band's second set included my first live version of "When it Rains it Pours," it also included a wink from the universe. Twiddle opened the set with "Earth Mama," a song they had played in Kansas City. But this time around, after the jam, the band slowed down the music and Mihali began to gently strum the beginnings of a new song. Usually I am able to identify the next song with a few opening chords, but this time I struggled to recognize the upcoming song. It turns out Twiddle was segueing into a cover song that they had never played before. This is referred to by music fans as a "bust out."

Unlike many jambands that only cover older songs of bands that no longer tour, Twiddle has broken new ground in recent years by boldly covering songs of their peers. In Kansas City, for example, Twiddle covered "Glory," an instrumental original by jamband Umphrey's McGee. Twiddle also recently covered "Son's Gonna Rise," a Citizen Cope song about a husband driving his pregnant wife to the hospital in the early morning hours as his wife begins labor. Interestingly, Citizen Cope appeared at The Wilma Theatre in Missoula the night before Twiddle played the Top Hat. Perhaps it was the Music Gods that arranged it so that Twiddle and their crew were in town to attend the Citizen Cope show.

On this night, Twiddle busted out "Round Here," a major hit of the Counting Crows with the talented Adam Duritz singing lead. Wait! What? Yes, that's right. Two nights before my

118

THE MUSIC GODS ARE REAL VOL. 1

plan to visit the Crow Tribe Reservation located just outside of Billings, Montana, on my "vision quest," Twiddle busted out a Counting Crows song. I was caught by surprise by this bust-out and deeply moved by the "Crow" synchronicity.

On the subject of the great band Counting Crows, their road to the show paralleled that of the Black Crowes. However, unlike the Black Crowes, the Counting Crows' story has a happy ending. Starting out, Duritz was in a band called the Himalayans. Thereafter in 1991, he formed a duo with producer/guitarist David Bryson. This relationship morphed into the full band that became known as Counting Crows. The name of the band was derived from "One for Sorrow," a British nursery rhyme about the superstitious counting of magpies, which happen to be members of the crow bird family.

Bryson used his production skills to record a demo tape for the band and before too long, they had a record deal and in 1993 recorded *August and Everything After*, their debut album. With breakthrough single "Mr. Jones," that album sold more than 7 million copies. In total, the band has sold more than 20 million albums on their road to the show and they are still together and touring. Counting Crows received mainstream music industry recognition with two Grammy Award nominations in 1994 for Best New Artist and Best Rock Performance by a Duo or Group with "Round Here," the song Twiddle covered in Missoula.

Just as Twiddle was finishing off an outstanding version of "Round Here" at the Top Hat, the band jammed right back into "Earth Mama" to finish off that song. The creativity of their setlists continued in the second set. After "Earth Mama>Round Here>Earth Mama," Twiddle blazed through

119

JONATHAN FINK

"Tiberius," a song about a medieval king's top knight who was too drunk to fight. Then they jammed into "Apples," flowed back into the next section of "Tiberius," went into "Funkytown," a cover song from the 1970s, and then jammed back to "Tiberius" to finish off the last portion of the song. It was a truly outstanding musicianship. During "Apples," Mihali and Gubb danced together in synch to the music, reminiscent of Trey Anastasio and Mike Gordon of Phish, who often jumped on trampolines and danced together when performing the song "You Enjoy Myself."

Near the end of the show, Twiddle played "Hattie's Jam," a song performed in memory of Mihali's dear friend Matthew Laconti, who died in a terrible car crash years ago. Usually Twiddle follows "Hattie's Jam" with the fan favorite "When it Rains it Pours," but this night the band did a fake out and played "Be There" instead. "Be There" is a beautiful, thoughtful song about friends and family who have passed on and become spirit guides and angels in the afterlife and look after those still living here on earth. After completing a straight-ahead version of "Be There," Twiddle did play "When it Rains it Pours" to finish off the encore. The crowd sang along with every word. As I listened to the meaningful lyrics sung by Mihali, I realized that he was right. My life is just fine. Now, each time I hear this song, I am reminded that problems do not stay with us. They get replaced by good news and happy times.

The show ended and I slowly strolled toward the exit with the rest of the crowd. I had a smile on my face thinking about the great day I'd had. Passing by the merchandise area again, I met the Iya Terra merch guy, talked with him for a few minutes, and bought a T-shirt. I told him tonight was my

THE MUSIC GODS ARE REAL VOL. 1

first Iya Terra show and I thought they were great and had a bright future in the business. I said that I was impressed with the band's musicianship, stage presence and the quality of the lyrics in their songs. I also gave him a signed copy of my *The Baseball Gods are Real* book.

The next day, driving the 300 miles from Missoula to Bozeman, I listened to Iya Terra's entire catalogue of music on Spotify, including *Full Circle*, their first album, and *Sacred Sound*, their follow-up release. Similar to my appreciation of Twiddle's songs and lyrics, because of their spiritual references, I found Iya Terra's music equally on point. About halfway to my destination, I stopped in Butte, Montana, for lunch. That's when I recalled Mihali telling me that the guys in Iya Terra were all vegetarians and some were also Rastafarians. It occurred to me right there that Iya Terra would be the perfect band to interview and write about in my next book in my music series, *The Music Gods are Real Volume. 2: The Religion of Music.*

Kevin Rondeau had previously invited me to watch the sound check at the Rialto, so I spent most of the rest of my day in Bozeman at the venue. Twiddle's sound check was particularly fun for me because the Kitchen Dwellers, a bluegrass jamband from Bozeman, were back in their hometown for a brief break from touring and had been invited by Twiddle to sit in at their show. During the Twiddle sound check, the band and the Kitchen Dwellers played "Hattibagen McRat," one of Twiddle's bluegrass songs, and then had a jam session. The best part of the jam may have occurred when the bands segued from a bluegrass jam into "Exodus," a Bob Marley song, blending bluegrass and reggae music together. It was awesome.

121

JONATHAN FINK

Then Twiddle and the Kitchen Dwellers filmed a promotional video for their upcoming show at the Red Rocks amphitheater, with the jamband Pigeons Playing Ping Pong also scheduled to perform. The members of both bands played ping pong together with guitars and banjos. It was hilarious.

After Twiddle completed its sound check, I stayed to watch the sound check of Iya Terra, the opening act and my new favorite reggae band. I watched the crew get set up and thoroughly enjoyed seeing Iya Terra play a few songs. Then, Brook Jordan, Twiddle's drummer, noticed that I was wearing a Stratton, Vermont, hoodie so he came over to introduce himself.

The Bozeman show was completely sold out. When Iya Terra came on stage to perform, you could feel the vibe and the excitement in the crowd. Although it was the band's first time playing in Montana and the crowd may not have been familiar with their songs, it did not matter. The contagious energy moved through the audience as Iya Terra played their favorite reggae songs including "Anti-Establishment," "Stars" and "Full Circle." Since I was now familiar with their material, I enjoyed this Iya Terra show even more than their impressive show the night before.

With the capacity crowd properly warmed up, Twiddle took the stage and played two outstanding sets of music. At one point, which was a highlight, the members of the Kitchen Dwellers joined Twiddle to play their songs "Vision of Mohr" and "Mountain." They also played Twiddle's "Hattibagen McRat" and for a few moments jammed Bob Marley's "Exodus" just as they had practiced during sound check. Other highlights from the show included "Beethoven and Greene" and "Frankenfoote," two of my favorite Twiddle songs.

Both nights in Montana, Ryan Dempsey stood up on his

small piano stool and played keyboards with his toes during the peak jams of "Tiberius" in Missoula and "Frankenfoote" in Bozeman. Yes, the same Ryan Dempsey who had recently broken his right leg and also hurt his back during the tour. Ryan Dempsey, may the Music Gods always be with you! The Twiddle performance in Bozeman was fabulous. And here is the setlist for that show.

Twiddle: 03/21/2019 - Rialto Theater, Bozeman, MT

I: Amydst The Myst> Doinkinbonk!!!, Syncopated Healing, Visions Of Mohr*, Hattibagen McRat*

II: Beethoven and Greene> Frankenfoote, Orderly Chaos> Beehop> Orderly Chaos, Every Soul

E: Mountain*, **

* w\ Kitchen Dwellers
**Exodus jam

When the show ended and the cheering died down, the house music came on. The first song played was "I Will Always Love You," by Whitney Houston. As the crowd lingered to celebrate this epic show, everybody was hugging each other other, knowing they had shared a great experience. I was reminded of "Scarlet Begonias," the Grateful Dead song that depicts strangers hugging strangers.

After the crowd filed out and the theater was empty, I went back to the merchandise table to say thank you and goodbye

JONATHAN FINK

to Kevin Rondeau. That's when Zdenek Gubb, Twiddle's bass player, came over and introduced himself. I said to Gubb, "Hey, I'm Fink, the author writing a book about you guys." Gubb smiled big and said, "Nice to meet you."

Before leaving the venue and heading back to my hotel, I went to the men's room. While washing my hands and face in the sink, I looked up to see a guy with a full head of dreadlocks standing next to me. When he cleared his dreads away from his face, I recognized him right away. It was Nick Loporchio, the bass player from Iya Terra.

Me being me, I introduced myself to Nick Loporchio and we got to talking. I told him how much I enjoyed their sets, both in Missoula and in Bozeman, and that I had given a signed book to their merchandise guy in Missoula. I mentioned my idea to interview Iya Terra for inclusion in the next book in my music series. I also mentioned how impressed I was to learn from Mihali that the guys in Iya Terra were vegetarians and some were even vegan. Discussing the theme of my next book, the religion of music, I told Loporchio that I thought it would be just perfect to interview a reggae band with members that were not just vegetarians, but also Rastafarians. He seemed receptive to the idea and I gave him the last signed copy of my first Baseball Gods book that I had in my backpack. We exchanged phone numbers and agreed to reconnect for an interview sometime after the winter tour was over.

The next day I drove to the Crow Tribe Reservation near Billings, Montana. It was a day I will never forget. I plan to write all about that truly surreal experience in my next book, *The Music Gods are Real - Volume 2: The Religion of Music.* After my visit to the Crow Tribe Reservation, I took a side trip

124

to see the Rimrocks, Montana's geological wonder of sandstone formations. On top of the Rimrocks, I enjoyed the view overlooking an enormous valley surrounded by mountains in the distance. The city of Billings sits in the valley below. I took out my yoga mat, found a quiet place to meditate and gave thanks to the Music Gods for this opportunity to see the beautiful state of Montana, interview Twiddle and visit the Crow Tribe Indian Reservation.

With the Rimrocks in my rearview mirror, I drove to Billings Logan International Airport to catch my flight back home to Kansas City. With some time to spare before heading to the gate area to board my flight, I went to the food court to buy a bottle of water. The woman behind the register at the food court wore a necklace. On it was both the Star of David and the Christian cross. Curious, I asked why the star and the cross? She replied that people forget that Jesus was a Jew and that we are all one.

CHAPTER TWENTY-ONE

The Road to Red Rocks

"Somewhere on the mountain, it's said that there's a potion, that makes you truly happy and infinite in wisdom."
— Twiddle

AFTER LEAVING THE BEAUTIFUL STATE OF MONTANA, Twiddle and its opening act Iya Terra played sold out shows the last two nights of the winter tour, one in Jackson Hole, Wyoming, and the other in Salt Lake City, Utah. A few days after the tour was over, I sent Nick Loporchio a text message to follow up on our discussion to schedule an interview. Unfortunately, after Iya Terra finished their tour with Twiddle, they continued right on to another tour with another reggae band. They spent the next month traveling up and down the East Coast, from Virginia to Vermont, and then back down again to finish the tour near where it started in North Carolina. Since Loporchio was still busy on tour, I suggested that we touch base again a few months later, after his tour and after I returned from the Twiddle show at the Red Rocks Amphitheatre.

126

THE MUSIC GODS ARE REAL VOL. 1

The Music Gods must have been working behind the scenes because Loporchio texted me that he too would be at Red Rocks to see the Twiddle show. As fate would have it, Iya Terra would be finishing their two months out on the road opening for reggae bands Steel Pulse and Stick Figure at Red Rocks on April 20th, 2019, just two weeks before Twiddle's show on May 2nd. Rather than do a phone interview, Loporchio and I agreed to do the interview in person when we were both in Colorado.

The Music Gods also arranged for me to join Twiddle on a portion of their weeklong Road to Red Rocks Tour, which the band would co-headline with Pigeons Playing Ping Pong. This tour was scheduled to begin just two days before my forty-fifth birthday in, of all places, Columbia, Missouri, a college town and home to the University of Missouri. Fortunately for me, this venue is only a two-hour drive from my hometown. During this short tour, each band would play a ninety-minute set, rotating the opener and the closer every night of the tour.

After playing the Blue Note in Columbia, the tour headed north to do a show at the Canopy Club in Urbana, Illinois, then trekked further north to play the Turner Hall Ballroom in Milwaukee, Wisconsin, and the Varsity Theater in Minneapolis, Minnesota. Finally, the tour traveled back down through the Midwest to play Omaha, Nebraska, before making the journey back across the great plains of Kansas to reach the Rocky Mountains of Colorado for their final stop of the tour — Red Rocks Amphitheatre. Personally, I was particularly excited to attend the first night of tour at the Blue Note because it would be the first time I would get to see Pigeons Playing Ping Pong perform live.

JONATHAN FINK

Pigeons Playing Ping Pong took their psychedelic funk music on road to the show in a manner similar to Twiddle's. Greg Ormont and Jeremy Schon, college freshmen at the University of Maryland, became friends and started playing music together in their dorm rooms. Then, just like Adam Duritz and David Bryson of the Counting Crows, they became an acoustic duo and started playing small gigs at coffee shops near their college campus. However, unlike the Counting Crows, who wrote and sang serious songs, Ormont and Schon got started with a focus on having fun and goofing off. Like Phish, they started with writing silly songs. When ready to take it to the next level, they added a drummer and bass player and formed a band. At that time, they turned a friend's garage into a rehearsal studio and, just like a car mechanic building an engine from scratch, they crafted their band's mission, musical style and sound. The group practiced and practiced until the band purred like a race car engine that was built to last. All they needed was a band name.

As the story goes, one day Ormont and Schon were sitting in their Psychology 100 class. Ormont was bored. In the Baltimore Sun article "Jam Fans Flock to Pigeons Playing Ping Pong," written by Sam Sessa, Ormont explains that he was just staring at a random page in his textbook when, in his zoned-out, trance-like state, a phrase from a paragraph flashed out at him and jumped off the page, with a gold light behind it. Ormont turned to Schon and said, "Hey man, this is our band name right here" to which Schon replied, "Sure." The four golden, magic words that ascended from his introduction to psychology textbook were — Pigeons Playing Ping Pong.

Pigeons Playing Ping Pong, like so many other jambands,

128

THE MUSIC GODS ARE REAL VOL. 1

ground on for years, slowly building up a loyal following of fans. They toured around the country and eventually established themselves as an "up-and-coming" jamband. As the years passed, their loyal fans earned the nickname "The Flock." With four self-released albums and logging an average 200 shows a year, the Pigeons have now reached the level of success where they are starting to sell out shows. Like Phish and Twiddle, the Pigeons have attained a big enough following to host *Domefest*, their own music festival. *Domefest* has been held in West Virginia for an impressive ten consecutive years. Unfortunately, I had been so immersed in Phish, Widespread Panic, Bruce Springsteen and Mumford & Sons for the last ten years, Pigeons Playing Ping Pong had not made it on to my music radar screen.

From time to time, I take notice of new concerts on the "latest release" tab on my Nugs music app on my iPhone. With a name like "Pigeons Playing Ping Pong," it was only a matter of time before I discovered the band and gave them a listen. While Twiddle dominated my music listening time recently, I did listen to a few Pigeons Playing Ping Pong shows along the way. Several of their songs got my attention including "Burning Up My Time," "Julia," "Horizon," "Pop Off," "Fun in Funk," "Melting Lights," "Ocean Flows" and "Schwanthem." I was particularly impressed when I heard the band's July 26, 2018, show that included an outstanding mash-up of two Phish songs, "Down with Disease" and "Run Like an Antelope."

After much anticipation, I left my hometown of Leawood, Kansas, and started driving east toward Columbia, Missouri. When I arrived at the Blue Note for the first night of the Road to Red Rocks Tour, I stopped by the merchandise table to

JONATHAN FINK

say hello to Kevin Rondeau. As we shook hands, I said, "It's my fourth show!" Knowing that four is our favorite number, Rondeau smiled big.

That night I watched the show from the balcony. At times I felt like an angel on a cloud, looking down from heaven, enjoying the music emanating from the stage. It actually reminded me of the floating meditation session I described in detail in my first book, *The Baseball Gods are Real*. During that deep meditation session, my first real "out of body experience," I felt as if I was floating like a cloud over Leawood watching my son Nate's baseball practice down below. While floating over the baseball field, it seemed as if I was able to control the direction that I wanted to fly. It was fantastic.

Back to the show at the Blue Note, lead singer Greg Ormont came on stage and said to the excited crowd, "Let's have some fun, alright?" While Twiddle's jamband foundation is arguably reggae-jam based, Pigeons Playing Ping Pong's foundation is funk-jam based. The Pigeons have developed a unique sound of high-energy psychedelic funk. Yet on this night, Pigeons opened up the show with a slow building jam that reminded me more of Phish than the funky Meters. Listening to this jam, I had flashbacks to my college days at Tulane where my friends and I listened to funk bands on the campus quad on many Friday afternoons. The Pigeons' performance that night of "Funk E. Zekiel" would have made bass player George Porter Jr. of the Meters proud! Eventually, the band transitioned and busted into a funky groove.

As Pigeons Playing Ping Pong transitioned from the quick little space jam and into the funk jam during the opening song, the audience below me started to move and groove to the

130

THE MUSIC GODS ARE REAL VOL. 1

music. Then, after the crowd seemed to fall into the trance of the opening jam, the band stopped playing simultaneously. They "froze," without moving, for some time, reminiscent of when the members of Phish sit still when they perform the song "Divided Sky." The Pigeons remained motionless, staring stage left up at the ceiling. The longer the band members stood still without moving, the louder and louder the audience cheered, hoping to break the Pigeons free from their orchestrated catatonic state. Then, without any signal, the band returned to the jam exactly where they had left off. It was a funny and entertaining moment. From a musicianship perspective, I was truly impressed.

I felt Pigeon's high energy and positive vibration right from the start of the show. It seemed that the members of the band were enjoying themselves just as much as their fans in the audience. And as the show went on, the magnetic individual personalities of the band members became self-evident. Pigeons' lead singer Greg Ormont looks a little bit like "Sideshow Bob," the character from the cartoon show *The Simpsons*, with his long curly hair. I suspect Ormont is well aware of the "cartoon image" that he portrays. I mean, the guy routinely wears colorful pajama pants while performing on stage. Pigeons' bass player Ben Carrey also likes to dress up for shows. One time I saw a video of a live Pigeons performance and Carrey was wearing a colorful Japanese kimono.

Not surprising for a band increasing speed on their way to the show, lead singer Ormont has amazing stage presence. The dude is just on fire while on stage. His personality is charismatic and likeable. He's a pure joy to watch. His facial expressions are hilarious and, at times, his eyes appear to be almost popping out of his head when he sings certain songs strumming his rhythm guitar. His energy cannot be contained. He is always moving around the stage, often jumping in the air, sometimes even spreading his legs in opposite directions as if he is doing a Michael Jordan basketball move. At times Ormont's carnival-like antics reminded me of "Krusty the Clown," another character from *The Simpsons*. Perhaps the best way for me to describe Ormont from a musical perspective is that he is the "Weird Al Yankovic" of the jamband scene.

I offer my personal descriptions of Greg Ormont as a compliment with the utmost respect. Remember, he is a performer, an artist, and, to a certain degree, an actor on stage. Obviously, I love what Pigeons Playing Ping Pong are doing and have been extremely impressed with their live shows and musicality. Beneath all the gimmicks and silly songs are four musicians that really know how to jam and put on a great show. They certainly did that night at the Blue Note, and here is their setlist for that performance.

Pigeons Playing Ping Pong: 4/24/2019 - The Blue Note, Columbia, MO

I: Funk E Zekiel, Melting Lights>Fox and Toad, Yo Soy Fiesta, Burning Up My Time>Offshoot>Pink Panther Theme>Offshoot, Fun in Funk, Poseidon, Snake Eyes, Landing, Ocean Flows

After seeing that show, I was more certain than ever that the future is bright for Pigeons Playing Ping Pong. I look forward

THE MUSIC GODS ARE REAL VOL. 1

to watching them travel further and further on their road to the show. PPPP, may the Music Gods always be with you!

Pigeons Playing Ping Pong was a hard act to follow but Twiddle was up to the task. Looking to match the high-energy vibrational tone set by Pigeons, the band delivered a creative set that showcased some of their more upbeat, lighthearted and fun songs. They avoided any slow songs or songs that focused on heavy subject matter, such as soul growth or overcoming life struggles. I think Twiddle was right on target with this approach to their set.

Twiddle opened their show with jam-friendly "Doinkinbonk!!" and wove that song together with other songs throughout the set. After "Doink," they jammed into "Beehop," the funky crowd favorite of many of their long-time fans. Then they moved back into "Doink." Then they jammed into "Nicodemus Portulay" before returning to "Doink" once again. It was tight. Then, with that great sequence behind them, the band moved forward with the rest of what turned out to be a truly entertaining show.

With only a few minutes left before curfew, there was no time for a long, extended jam to finish off the show. However, Twiddle left the crowd with something better, wisdom and inspiration. Twiddle finished the show with a cover of "Barbeque," a song by the band Animal Liberation Orchestra, also known as "ALO." Mihali sang the following lyrics:

The road is long and windy, full of twists and turns.
But before you can rise from the ashes,
you've got to burn baby burn.
Welcome to your barbecue, pig out and dream anew.

Here's the setlist for Twiddle's outstanding performance that night.

Twiddle: 04/24/2019 – The Blue Note, Columbia, MO

I: Doinkinbonk!!!> Beehop> Doinkinbonk!!!> Nicodemus Portulay> Doinkinbonk!!!, Second Wind> Zazu's Flight> Polluted Beauty, Brown Chicken Brown Cow

E: Barbeque

After the show at the Blue Note, the crews packed up their gear and the tour buses headed off on their road to Red Rocks, with a few stops along the way. The highlight of the performance in Urbana, Illinois, occurred when all the members of Pigeons Playing Ping Pong joined Twiddle for the encore and played the fun and spooky song "Ghostbusters." Then there was some "Milwaukee Madness" at the sold-out show at the Turner Ballroom in Wisconsin. During the Twiddle song "Apples," Pigeons' bass player Ben Carrey joined Twiddle for the jam. As he started to play his slide whistle, the venue's security guards thought he was a random fan trying to get on stage, apprehended him from behind, and carried him off stage right. Then later in the show, Mihali came on stage wearing pajama pants and joined Pigeons for the song "Live It Up." As a goof, Twiddle's bass player Zdenek Gubb, dressed in a yellow security vest, came on stage, grabbed Mihali from behind by surprise and carried him off stage!

Before the tour moved on to another sold-out show in

THE MUSIC GODS ARE REAL VOL. 1

Minneapolis, there was one more funny moment in Milwaukee. When the Pigeons took the stage, "Gator," their drummer, wore a black and green trimmed Milwaukee Bucks basketball visitor's jersey. As he reached center stage, the crowd cheered loudly for the reference to their beloved home team. Then, to everyone's surprise, Gator took off this jersey and revealed a Milwaukee Bucks white, home jersey that he was wearing underneath. The home crowd cheered again and roared even louder to show their approval. Perhaps the Music Gods were sending Mihali a message to wear the Royals baseball jersey that I had given him the next time Twiddle plays Kansas City.

Perhaps the most memorable moment of the April 27, 2019, show in Minneapolis occurred when Pigeons' lead guitarist Jeremy Schon, who is Jewish, sat in with Twiddle for the song "Mad World." Maybe it was a coincidence, but earlier in the day, which happened to be the last day of Passover, a very meaningful Jewish holiday, an angry, hateful, crazed 19-year-old man entered a synagogue during services in San Diego, California. Without warning, he opened fire with a gun, killing an innocent victim. A female congregant jumped in front of the rabbi, saving his life, but by doing so, gave up her own. The rabbi said in an interview the next day that the terrible tragedy had a miracle moment. As the gunman opened fire, his gun jammed, preventing him from firing any more bullets and increasing the death toll. Shortly thereafter, the terrorist was apprehended by police. As I said, "Mad World" was a fitting song choice for Twiddle to sing with Jeremy Schon.

It is a mad world indeed. We live on a planet with free will where both darkness and light exist. The spiritual battle between good and evil and darkness and light rages on now

135

more than ever. There is an old saying, "Darkness scatters when a candle is lit." Thus, darkness only exists in the absence of light. I will explore this subject in more detail in my next book, *The Music Gods are Real - Volume 2: The Religion of Music*. I believe that one of the best ways to spread love and light is through music. And what better place exists for me to cultivate more love and light to share with others than at my first visit to the mecca of music — Red Rocks Amphitheatre.

Red Rocks is an open-air amphitheater ten miles west of Denver. The venue is essentially embedded in a mountainside. There is a large disc-shaped rock behind the stage, a huge vertical rock angled outward from stage right and several large rock formations on stage left. The venue is surrounded by the natural beauty of Red Rocks Mountain Park and the amphitheater seats 9,525. Geologically, the rocks surrounding the venue are tinted red and remind me of the rock structures of the magnificent Garden of the Gods in Colorado Springs. Perhaps there is some spiritual connection between the two places because the area now known as "Red Rocks" was originally known as "The Garden of the Angels."

In the jamband community, headlining a show at Red Rocks is equivalent to making it big on the road to the show. The Beatles played Red Rocks in 1964. Simon & Garfunkel played Red Rocks in 1967. Jimi Hendrix played Red Rocks in 1968. Jamband Widespread Panic holds the record for most sold-out shows at the venue with an impressive 54 as of 2018. That's 54 sold-out shows!

Perhaps the reason that Red Rocks is considered sacred in the jamband community is because it was one of the favorite venues of the greatest jamband of all time, the Grateful Dead.

THE MUSIC GODS ARE REAL VOL. 1

While playing Red Rocks signifies making it on the road to the show for most musicians, it has the same significance for music fans and now I understand why. Red Rocks is the most beautiful music venue I have ever seen. It is simply majestic.

After picking up my ticket at will call (thanks again to Kevin Rondeau and Dan Travis), I parked my car in the lower lot and began my sacred music pilgrimage. Leaving the parking lot, I joined the fans walking uphill on a long road leading to the venue. As I hiked and started to get a bit tired, I turned to another fan walking right next to me and joked about the strenuous walk and said, "It's almost like a rite of passage." The guy laughed and said, "For sure, but the real sacrifice is still to come." When we finally reached a huge stair-case, I knew what the guy was talking about. The staircase up to the gates to the amphitheater was long, very steep, and almost straight-up vertical. Halfway up these steep steps, I heard a fan say to her friend, "You see, this is why I do all that yoga. That warrior two pose is coming in handy right about now." I laughed, made eye contact with the girls, smiled and said to them, bowing with respect from one yogi to another, "Namaste."

I entered the glorious venue and immediately understood why this place is so revered. Just like the Garden of the Gods, the Red Rocks Amphitheatre literally looks like it was built by the hands of god, or perhaps angels with a great appreciation for music. The stage sits at the bottom of a hill and the towering rocks circle all around the venue, protecting it from wind and ensuring great acoustics. The acoustics in this natural setting are of such high quality that opera singers performing at the Red Rocks in the early 1900s did so without microphones.

The singers could be heard at the top of the venue perfectly. On this night, not only were the natural design and acoustics perfect, so too was the weather. I think the Music Gods may have had something to do with that.

About ten days before the show, I checked the weather report on my iPhone for Morrison, Colorado. The long-term forecast called for rain the day of the show and there even was a prediction for snow the day before the show. I posted on Twitter, Instagram, and Facebook, jokingly asking the Music Gods for help, "Dear Music Gods, after scheduled rain in Morrison, CO, on Monday, Tuesday and Wednesday next week, please make next Thursday a day of sunshine and a night of twinkling stars. I thank you." Like the Native Americans who performed rain dances asking their medicine fathers to make it rain, I was asking the Music Gods to prevent the rain and snow. Coincidence or not, just two days later, the forecast for the day of the show improved dramatically. I posted, "*The Road to Red Rocks* Weather Update: Dear Music Gods, Well done! I am grateful. Please keep up the good work. Thank you! Fink." Two days closer to the show, the forecast called for sunny skies for both Thursday and Friday. I posted my thanks on social media saying, "*The Road to Red Rocks* weather update for this Thursday. Forecast > sunny skies by day and twinkling stars at night. The Music Gods are Real. I am grateful."

The most recent forecast turned out to be accurate. With sunny skies and a gentle breeze, thanks to the Music Gods, the final show of the Road to Red Rocks Tour was set to begin. The Kitchen Dwellers were the opening act. Their "Road to Red Rocks" had started many years before, in 2010, in the beautiful state of Montana. Like many of the bands I highlight

THE MUSIC GODS ARE REAL VOL. 1

in this book, the roots of the Kitchen Dwellers took hold on a college campus. In this instance, it was at Montana State University in Bozeman.

This band from Montana broke new ground with a focus on jam-oriented bluegrass music. While many novice music fans may have an image of bluegrass music being casually played with banjos and fiddles, on a back porch, with pink lemonade being sipped somewhere out in the mountains with the setting sun going down, the Kitchen Dwellers quickly dispel that myth. The band has crafted a high energy, fast-paced style of bluegrass music that some would describe as psychedelic. And live on stage, the Kitchen Dwellers love to jam.

Music critics, always looking to label bands, have called the Kitchen Dwellers' style of music "newgrass" or "jamgrass," but some of their fans would describe it as "galaxy grass." Other "newgrass" bands include Greensky Bluegrass, Billy Strings, Yonder Mountain String Band, Railroad Earth and the Infamous Stringdusters. It is possible that the bluegrass revival started with the emergence of the String Cheese Incident, a jamband from Colorado with a foundation in bluegrass music. While String Cheese Incident may have plowed the snow off the Rocky Mountain roads for bands like the Kitchen Dwellers, the quartet from Bozeman has paved the way for others who wish to travel down the "jamgrass" road. Like the String Cheese Incident, the Kitchen Dwellers shine in a live music setting.

I was very impressed with the Kitchen Dwellers' opening set at Red Rocks right from the start. This bluegrass-jam quartet can absolutely shred. With just four acoustic instruments, the banjo, mandolin, acoustic guitar and stand-up bass, this band

JONATHAN FINK

can build up a jam with the best of them. And the Red Rocks crowd was face-melted into a frenzy several times during their performance. The Kitchen Dwellers displayed tight musicianship, unique pedal sound effects, and fabulous improvisational jamming. There was no doubt in my mind that this band was bound for greatness.

Even as the opening band, I could tell that the Kitchen Dwellers had a unique group of loyal fans at the show. You could easily pick them out of the crowd, because many of them were wearing white kitchen aprons over their clothes, like a chef working behind the counter in the back of a restaurant. Their performance that night had many highlights including their rendition of "Gypsy," during which they broke into a "reggae jam" that would have made reggae legend Bob Marley proud. During another jam during the set, Torrin Daniels turned on a sound effect that made his banjo sound just like Jerry Garcia of the Grateful Dead. It was awesome.

The Kitchen Dwellers interwove many tight jams throughout their set. Perhaps their most outstanding jam came during "Mountain," their set closer. Not only did "Mountain" have the most triumphant jam of the set, the song also brought with it some inspirational lyrics. As I listened and sang along to the chorus, "I wish I was a mountain, so strong in my resolve, I wish I was a mountain, cause I would stand my ground and never fall," I thought about my spiritual path, how far I had come, and how far I still need to go. After a glorious jam that included some reggae, some bluegrass and even a Jerry Garcia-themed jam, the band worked its way back into the chorus of the song.

The Kitchen Dwellers played a flawless set of outstanding music. The band's first show at Red Rocks was most certainly a success. With great songs, amazing musicianship, and the

140

THE MUSIC GODS ARE REAL VOL. 1

ability to jam, there was no doubt in my mind that the road to the show for the Kitchen Dwellers would be filled with much success in the years to come. It's only a matter of time before they will headline Red Rocks themselves. Kitchen Dwellers, may the Music Gods always be with you!

Speaking of bands that will soon be hosting and headlining their own concerts at Red Rocks, up next on stage after the Kitchen Dwellers was Pigeons Playing Ping Pong. They began their set with "Poseidon," a song that sounds like it should be on a Disney movie soundtrack with its happy, fun, island-like sound. The band jammed out this song, commanding the attention of the audience, and made it clear to the Colorado crowd that they were a very legit jamband. The crowd was mesmerized by the band's first jam and you could tell that Pigeons, like Twiddle, was on the verge of jamband great-ness. Several times during their set, their jams reached levels of thrilling proportions. Towards the end of the set, I looked around at the crowd and the venue was absolutely filled with happy, dancing hippies.

Many in the crowd were clearly die-hard fans of the Pigeons. The band's fanbase, just like the band they love, displayed a vivacious collective personality, reminiscent of passionate, quirky Phish fans. Here is one example of the awesomeness of "the Flock." During the show, these fans threw ping pong balls into the air, similar to Phish fans who throw glow sticks in the air. I actually caught a ping pong ball bouncing my way, held it up to take a closer look, and noticed that the words on the ball identified where the fans travelled from for this show. This ball was labelled "Wyoming Flock." I was very impressed with the distance these fans traveled to see the Pigeons perform, and here is the setlist they got to see that night.

141

JONATHAN FINK

Pigeons Playing Ping Pong: 5/02/2019 – Red Rocks
Amphitheatre, Morrison, CO

I: Poseidon, Yo Soy Fiesta, Somethin' For Ya> Kiwi> Distant
Times, Sunny Day, Walk Outside> Sir Real> Walk Outside,
Melting Lights> The Liquid, Ocean Flows

Having played fun and light-hearted setlists throughout
the prior week, Twiddle changed direction and played an
emotional set at this last show of tour on the sacred ground of
Red Rocks. Twiddle opened their show with the meaningful
song "Hattie's Jam," which had special significance for me.

The day before leaving for Denver, I emailed Kevin
Rondeau and asked for Hattibagen's real name so that I could
in some small way memorialize him in the Music Gods book I
was in the process of writing. Rondeau replied with the name
Matthew Laconti. Shortly thereafter, while driving in my
car to run some errands, I thought about the Twiddle songs
that impacted me the most. They were the songs that Mihali
had written about his dear friend Matthew. Matthew's death
created suffering for Mihali, who used music and songwriting
to overcome his emotional pain. Those songs also helped me
through a difficult time. My next thought was that I should
actually dedicate the book to Matthew Laconti.

It had been raining all day in Kansas City. After the rain
stopped, I looked up into the sky and saw the biggest, most
beautiful rainbow hovering over my house. I knew that the
Music Gods had just sent me a sign that dedicating my book to
Mihali's dear friend was the right thing to do. I sent Rondeau
and Dan Travis an email, including a photo of the rainbow

142

THE MUSIC GODS ARE REAL VOL. 1

and asked them to tell Savoulidis about dedicating this book to his buddy.

Starting with "Hattie's Jam," Twiddle played a flawless set of music that night at Red Rocks. No extra special improvisational jams were needed on this night since songs like "Jamflowman," "Tiberius" and "Frankenfoote" all had dynamic and euphoric instrumental segments embedded within. Twiddle, too, left the stage to the sound of screaming fans. Here is their setlist for the evening.

Twiddle: 5/02/2019 – Red Rocks Amphitheatre, Morrison, CO

I: Hatti's Jam> The Box> Grandpa Fox> When It Rains It Pours, Tiberius, Subconscious Prelude (1), Jamflowman> Dinner Fork> Frankenfoote, Be There

Twidgeon Dwellers: 5/02/2019 – Red Rocks Amphitheatre, Morrison, CO

I: Apples (2,3), Visions Of Mohr (4), I'm Gonna Be (500 Miles) (2,3) F.U. (2,3) Psycho Killer (3), The Sound of Silence (5), Bohemian Rhapsody (6,4,3)

1.w\ Richard Vagner
2.w\ Torrin Daniels (KD)
3.w\ Pigeons Playing Ping Pong
4.w\ Kitchen Dwellers
5.Savoulidis & Ormont
6.w\ Denver Choir League

JONATHAN FINK

After three outstanding sets of music from the Kitchen Dwellers, Pigeons Playing Ping Pong and Twiddle, all three bands came back on stage to form a super ensemble, appropriately named "Twidgeon Dwellers," that really stole the show. Highlights of this fourth set included cover songs "I'm Gonna Be (500 Miles)" by the Proclaimers and the Talking Heads' "Psycho Killer." The first surprise of the encore set occurred when Mihali from Twiddle and Ormont from Pigeons sang Simon & Garfunkel's "The Sounds of Silence" a cappella. The epic evening came to a triumphant close when the combined bands were joined by the Denver Choir League for a sensational version of Queens' "Bohemian Rhapsody."

Throughout the show, I looked for Twiddle's manager Kevin Rondeau to say hello and thank him. I finally found him after the show ended as he emerged from the crowd and walked my way. I told him that I thought the show was awesome and his band had done the Red Rocks proud.

As amazing as this day was at Red Rocks, my Music God adventures in Colorado were not over yet. Before I flew back to Kansas City the next day, I had the opportunity to sit down and interview Nick Loporchio from reggae band — Iya Terra. My pre-interview research revealed that Iya Terra's road to the show began like Pigeons Playing Ping Pong, with two good friends who both happened to love music. However, unlike the Black Crowes or the Counting Crows, who launched their music careers by recording a demo tape, Nathan Aurora and Nick Loporchio started out in a fashion similar to Patti Rothberg. However, rather than playing in the dark and dirty subway stations of New York City like Rothberg, Aurora and Loporchio, who originally met on craigslist, began their

144

THE MUSIC GODS ARE REAL VOL. 1

careers playing their music on streets and sidewalks lined with palm trees near the campus of UCLA.

Loporchio met Aurora after Aurora moved to Los Angeles from Las Vegas in 2013. At the time, Loporchio was a pre-med student and envisioned himself becoming an orthopedic surgeon and Aurora was an English major still looking to find his life purpose. After spending time together and becoming friends, they went to see the reggae band SOJA together. As they walked out of that SOJA show, their vision for their new band came into view.

Loporchio and Aurora decided to form a reggae band with the mission to change the world for the better by spreading a message of unity, love, respect and spiritual awakening. They developed their own unique sound of upbeat, conscious, high vibration reggae music. They chose the band name "Iya Terra" because it means "higher ground." In their case, higher ground refers to a moral or ethical position of advantage or superiority, and a perfect name choice for a band with anti-establishment political views. A year later, in 2014, Iya Terra recorded their first album.

With a meaningful band name, a new reggae sound, and a mission to change the world, Iya Terra embarked on their first tour. Since they did not have a band manager yet, they self-managed. With a newly recorded disc to promote, Loporchio and Aurora organized and promoted their own tour joined by their reggae friends Ital Vibes. They called it the *Link Up Tour*. Staying true to their Rastafarian beliefs, Iya Terra remained grateful, humble and retained their faith in a "higher power" as they began their road to the show. Not surprisingly, the tour was a success.

JONATHAN FINK

Like all good manifestors, Iya Terra had big dreams and visualized it. In the 2015 article "A Look Inside Iya Terra," written by Andrew Chu at Top Shelf Reggae, lead singer Aurora said, "I can probably speak for the whole band when I say that 2014 was the best year of our lives, haha. It was nothing short of a manifestation of our dreams. In 2013, we were just putting the band together and thinking 'man it would be so sick to play some festivals, share the stage with our favorite artists, and get out on tour,' and in 2014 we were able to do that. Definitely really blessed."

While I look forward to meeting Nathan Aurora one day, the next person the Music Gods directed me to interview for my music book series was Iya Terra's bass player — Nick Loporchio. Loporchio and I agreed to meet at a small house near Commerce City, Colorado, where he was staying. The place was not too far from Dick's Sporting Goods Park, where Phish plays three shows every Labor Day Weekend. When I arrived, Loporchio and two of his friends were hanging out in the backyard, enjoying the fresh air of another beautiful Colorado morning. Just like the day before, the sun was shining, a few clouds casually floated across the sky, and there was a cool, gentle breeze in the air.

Loporchio and I spent an hour together chatting and sharing some of our life experiences mixed in between the interview questions I had previously prepared. Loporchio discussed his recent eight weeks out on tour and told me a story that he said I could write about in my book and share with my readers.

On their most recent tour, Iya Terra performed in Montreal, Canada. Since Canada had recently passed legislation making marijuana legal for recreational use, the band loaded up on supplies for the rest of their travels. They had no problems with the border guards while crossing back into the United States, but between the Canadian border and Buffalo, New York, Iya Terra's tour bus was stopped by police. Loporchio described the police stop in detail because the search that ensued became particularly troublesome.

The tour bus was pulled over by New York State troopers. After a few questions and a quick perusal, a trooper asked everyone on the bus to get out. The police proceeded to search the bus for hours, from darkness to daylight, while the band members and their crew stood alongside the highway with cars whizzing by at high speeds. First, the troopers found a large stash of marijuana. Shortly thereafter, another trooper came out of the bus, looking like he had just won the jackpot, and things started to go from bad to worse.

The trooper held a plastic bag up in the air and shined his flashlight right on the bag for everyone to clearly see. Inside the bag were "magic mushrooms," a psychedelic drug that grows naturally from the earth just like the marijuana plant. However, unlike marijuana, which is legal in almost half of the country these days for medical or recreational purposes, magic mushrooms are still, at least for now, very illegal.

The police officer holding the bag of mushrooms said, "Ok, now we have a problem. Who does this belong to?" Loporchio bravely raised his hand right away and replied, "It's mine." Behind his long dreadlocks and beard, Loporchio hoped the trooper would see a warm, friendly smile and the handsome face of an honest man.

The smile, the face and the honesty won the day. While the police officers made Iya Terra dump all of their magic

JONATHAN FINK

mushrooms and cannabis into the forest and gave them a stern warning, they did not arrest them or file any criminal charges. As the State Troopers were leaving, one of them told Loporchio and his bandmates that they were free to go. He told them that the only reason this situation ended well was because of Loporchio's honesty.

After Loporchio told this tale, I decided to direct the interview to a somewhat related subject. Speaking of "mushrooms," I told Loporchio I was a vegetarian and asked him when and how he became one. On this subject, Loporchio had another mind-blowing story to tell and again gave me permission to share it. A few years ago, he was experimenting with magic mushrooms with his friends. After a while, not feeling the effects, he decided to eat a lot more. When the first and second helpings of the magic mushrooms began to kick in, he began to hallucinate. During his mushroom trip, he became a cow. Not just a cow, but the specific cow that provided the steak that he had eaten for dinner the night before. Loporchio became sick to his stomach. Then he channeled the thoughts and feelings of that cow, the animal that was murdered in a factory and chopped up into pieces for human consumption. The images in his mind were so real that he could not stop vomiting. Loporchio said that it was such a bad trip that he never ate meat again.

Continuing the interview, I was pleased to learn that Loporchio practiced yoga and meditation. In fact, while recording their first EP, on a small budget with limited time in the recording studio, the band meditated together before each recording. They wanted to make sure that each take was perfect.

THE MUSIC GODS ARE REAL VOL. 1

After talking about vegetarianism, yoga and meditation, Loporchio and I discussed the idea of manifesting our thoughts into reality. He and his bandmates were very familiar with the concept. Loporchio explained that they used Feng Shui, one of the five arts of Chinese metaphysics, to design their rehearsal studio because it is known to harmonize the energetic forces for individuals and their surrounding environments regardless of location. The band made sure to have natural sunlight and access to fresh air and they placed furniture and equipment in spots that best permitted the "qi" energy to flow. In short, they designed their rehearsal studio to help them manifest a successful music career.

With this information, it became clear to me that Iya Terra had literally manifested their music career dreams to come true. Like those manifestors who use vision boards to visualize their life goals, the band also hung two inspirational posters on their rehearsal studio wall. As I discussed in my first publication, *The Baseball Gods are Real*, I did the same thing as a teenager by hanging a Black Crowes poster on my bedroom wall and eventually toured with Patti Rothberg and the Crowes in Europe in 1997.

Loporchio told me that the first poster on the wall in their studio was a picture of the Red Rocks Amphitheatre with the reggae band Steel Pulse performing live on stage. The second poster was a picture of the main stage at the California Roots Music & Arts Festival, nicknamed "The Bowl." Each day at rehearsal, the band would daydream about one day playing at Red Rocks and on the main stage at the Roots Festival. They also dreamed of one day playing shows with their reggae heroes Steel Pulse and SOJA.

JONATHAN FINK

Now here is where things get fascinating. Just six years after forming the band, Iya Terra made it on their road to the show by performing at Red Rocks on April 20, 2019, just as they had manifested. The Music Gods manipulated this performance so that Iya Terra would share the stage with their friends Stick Figure and their reggae idols — Steel Pulse. A few months later, Iya Terra went to California for the Roots Festival and performed for the first time at — The Bowl. Lastly, after Iya Terra finished their winter tour with Twiddle, they toured for a month up and down the East Coast with none other than — SOJA. I think Nick Loporchio would agree with me that — The Music Gods are Real!

THE CONCLUSION

"Right here right now, that's exactly where I want to be."
— Iya Terra

IN *THE MUSIC GODS ARE REAL: VOLUME I - THE ROAD TO the Show*, I take my readers along for the ride as I continue on my spiritual path, this time with music as my guide. This book also chronicles the music road to the show for Bruce Springsteen and the E Street Band, Phish, Widespread Panic, the Grateful Dead, Mumford & Sons, the Black Crowes, the Counting Crows, Scarecrow Collection, Patti Rothberg, the Primitive Radio Gods, Pigeons Playing Ping Pong, the Kitchen Dwellers, Iya Terra and of course Twiddle.

As you might have guessed, I use "the road to the show" as a metaphor for life. "The Show" is symbolic for achieving goals, whatever they may be. The road is not flat or straight. There will be ups and downs along the way. But whether you are a minor league baseball player, a musician, a financial advisor or whatever else you might aspire to be in life, you will learn from every accomplishment and setback and keep moving forward on your own road to the show. May the Music Gods always be with you!

THE ACKNOWLEDGEMENTS

To Reggie Fink, The Soulmate

To Kayla Fink, The Angel Girl

To Nate Fink, The Divided Sky

To Beth and Jeffrey Fink, The Music Lovers

To Twiddle, The 2019 Winter Tour

To Kevin Rondeau, The Number Four

To Daniel Travis, The Best Friend

To Mihai Savoulidis, The White Light

To Ryan Dempsey, The Orlando's Bar

To Zdenek Gubb, The Doinkinbonk!!!

To Brook Jordan, The Second Wind

To Kyle Travis, The Artist

To Eric Milano, The Megatudes

To Alicia Gelernt, The Boss

To Tony Shimkin, The Producer

JONATHAN FINK

To Patti Rothberg, The Electric Lady

To Larry Braverman, The EMI Summer Internship

To Bruce Springsteen & the E Street Band, The Promised Land

To the Spin Doctors and Blues Traveler, The Wetlands

To Scarecrow Collection, The Crossroads

To the Black Crowes, The 1997 European Tour

To Phish, The Clifford Ball

To Widespread Panic, The Driving Song

To the Grateful Dead, The Music Never Stopped

To Russ, The Wolf

To Mumford and Sons, The Road to Red Rocks

To Iya Terra, The Road to Montana

To Nick Loporchio, The Interview

To Pigeons Playing Ping Pong, The Flock

To the Primitive Radio Gods, The Patti Rothberg Tour

To the Kitchen Dwellers, The Mountain

To Counting Crows, The Cover Song

To the Wiggles, The Big Red Car

To Alex Lavigne, The recordBar Prophecy

To Dr. Minor, The Bruce Fan

To Mark Weinberg and Matthew Sechter, The Spin Doctors

To Jeroen de Wit, The Past Life Regressionist

To Dolores Cannon, The Method

To Mike and Lauren Lee, The Crow Tribe and The Seeker

THE MUSIC GODS ARE REAL VOL. 1

To the Crow Tribe of Montana, The Vision Quest
To Meg Schader, The Editor
To Meg Reid, The Book Cover and Book Layout Designer
To Kim Watson, The Biography Picture
To Abi Laksono, The Polo Grounds Publishing Logo
To Allen Galton, The Electronic Mandolin Player

In Loving Memory of

Lori Kaye, The Hero

Lori Kaye was at a synagogue in San Diego on April 27, 2019, to mourn her mother. She was killed while protecting the rabbi from an anti-Semitic gunman who attacked the synagogue on the last day of Passover.

In Loving Memory of Sharon Greenwood, The Classical Music Lover.

JULY 23, 2018
Los Angeles, CA
Jonathan Fink and Jeroen de Wit

JONATHAN FINK

FEBRUARY 4, 2019
The recordBar - Kansas City, MO
Mihali Savoulidis and Jonathan Fink

THE MUSIC GODS ARE REAL VOL. 1

MARCH 22, 2019
Billings Logan International Airport

MAY 2, 2019
Red Rocks Amphitheatre - Morrison, CO
Kitchen Dwellers

THE MUSIC GODS ARE REAL VOL. 1

MAY 2, 2019
Red Rocks Amphitheatre - Morrison, CO
Ryan Dempsey

JONATHAN FINK

MAY 2, 2019
Red Rocks Amphitheatre, Morrison, CO
TwidGeon Dwellers with Denver Choir League

THE MUSIC GODS ARE REAL VOL. 1

MAY 2, 2019
Red Rocks Amphitheatre - Morrison, CO
Kevin Rondeau and Jonathan Fink

JONATHAN FINK

MAY 3, 2019
Denver, CO
Nick "Porch" Loporchio and Jonathan Fink

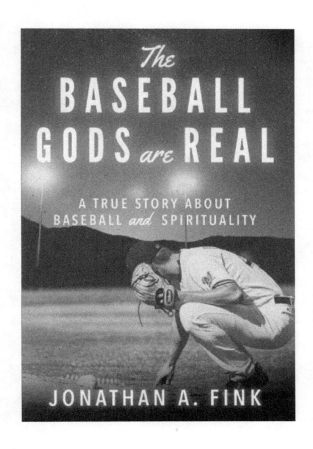

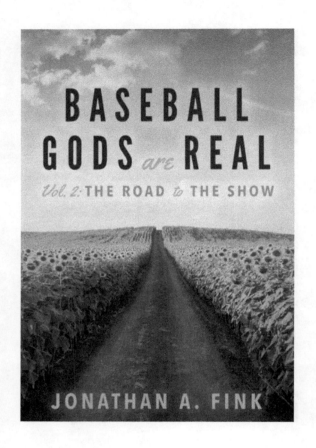

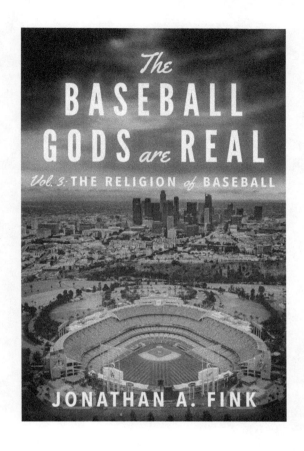

CPSIA information can be obtained
at www.ICGtesting.com
Printed in the USA
BVHW071737080720
583177BV00001B/65/J